Math Workshop in Action

Find out how Math Workshops engage students and increase learning. This practical book from bestselling author Dr. Nicki Newton explains why Math Workshops are effective and gives you step-by-step instructions for implementing and managing your own workshop.

You'll find out how to . . .

- create a math-rich environment;
- use anchor charts effectively;
- manage the workshop;
- begin a workshop with activities;
- lead whole-group mini-lessons;
- make workstations meaningful and engaging;
- create guided math groups;
- implement "the Share" effectively; and
- ensure balanced assessments.

Each chapter offers a variety of charts and tools that you can use in the classroom immediately, as well as reflection questions and key points. The book also features a handy Quick-Start Guide to help you as you implement your own workshop.

Dr. Nicki Newton has been an educator for 27 years, working both nationally and internationally, with students of all ages. She has worked on developing Math Workshop and Guided Math Institutes around the country. She is also an avid blogger (www.guidedmath.wordpress.com) and Pinterest pinner (https://www.pinterest.com/drnicki7/).

Other Eye On Education Books Available from Routledge

(www.routledge.com/eyeoneducation)

**Guided Math in Action: Building Each Student's
Mathematical Proficiency with Small-Group Instruction**
Dr. Nicki Newton

**Math Running Records in Action: A Framework
for Assessing Basic Fact Fluency**
Dr. Nicki Newton

**Using Children's Literature to Teach Problem Solving
in Math: Addressing the Common Core in K–2**
Jeanne White

**The Common Core Grammar Toolkit: Using Mentor
Texts to Teach the Language Standards in Grades 3–5**
Sean Ruday

**The Informational Writing Toolkit:
Using Mentor Texts in Grades 3–5**
Sean Ruday

**Close Reading in Elementary School:
Bringing Readers and Texts Together**
Diana Sisson and Betsy Sisson

**Infusing Grammar into the Writer's Workshop:
A Guide for Teachers in Grades K–8**
Amy Benjamin and Barbara Golub

Vocabulary Strategies That Work: Do This—Not That!
Lori G. Wilfong

Nonfiction Strategies That Work: Do This—Not That!
Lori G. Wilfong

Writing Strategies That Work: Do This—Not That!
Lori G. Wilfong

Family Math Night: Math Standards in Action
Jennifer Taylor-Cox

Family Reading Night, Second Edition
Darcy J. Hutchins, Joyce L. Epstein, Marsha D. Greenfield

Family Science Night: Fun Tips, Activities, and Ideas
Shelley Connell

Math Workshop in Action

Strategies for Grades K–5

Dr. Nicki Newton

Routledge
Taylor & Francis Group

NEW YORK AND LONDON

First published 2016
by Routledge
711 Third Avenue, New York, NY 10017

and by Routledge
2 Park Square, Milton Park, Abingdon, Oxon, OX14 4RN

Routledge is an imprint of the Taylor & Francis Group, an informa business

Library of Congress Cataloging-in-Publication Data
Newton, Nicki.
   Math workshop in action : strategies for grades K–5 / by Nicki Newton.
      pages cm
   Includes bibliographical references.
   1. Mathematics—Study and teaching (Elementary)   2. Elementary school teachers—Training of.   3. Mathematics teachers—Training of.   I. Title.
      QA107.2.N49 2015
      372.7—dc23
      2015004470

ISBN: 978-1-138-78587-8 (pbk)
ISBN: 978-1-315-76759-8 (ebk)

Typeset in Palatino and Formata
by Apex CoVantage, LLC

Dedication

I dedicate this book to the schools I work in every day. It is an honor to work with you. I also dedicate this book to my mom and dad and grandparents; I stand on your shoulders.

Contents

Meet the Author

Dr. Nicki Newton has been an educator for 27 years, working both nationally and internationally, with students of all ages. Having spent the first part of her career as a literacy and social studies specialist, she built on those frameworks to inform her math work. She believes that math is intricately intertwined with reading, writing, listening and speaking. She has worked on developing Math Workshop and Guided Math Institutes around the country. Most recently, she has been helping districts and schools nationwide to integrate their State Standards for Mathematics and think deeply about how to teach these within a Math Workshop Model. Dr. Nicki works with teachers, coaches and administrators to make math come alive by considering the powerful impact of building a community of mathematicians who make meaning of real math together. When students do real math, they learn it. They own it, they understand it, and they can do it. Every one of them. Dr. Nicki is also an avid blogger (www.guidedmath.wordpress .com) and Pinterest pinner (https://www.pinterest.com/drnicki7/).

Acknowledgments

It is impossible to write a book alone. I thank so many people. First, I thank my family. I love them and they support me and cheer me on (to name a few: Tia, Marvin, Uncle Bill, Sharon & Clinese). Next, I thank Brittany, who allows me to make it happen. Best assistant ever! I also thank Derek, best advisor ever! I thank my entire staff (including Anna, Nancy, Daniel & John). I couldn't do it without my friends telling me that I can write however many books I want (Kimberly, Tracie & Tammy). I thank my editor Lauren, who is ever patient and helpful.

I thank the teachers and the students I work with every day who allow me to teach and learn with them along this journey. I thank PS 138 (Mrs. Dawkins, Mrs. Fleshman, Mrs. Jimenez, Mrs. Hargett, & Mrs. Owens & the entire staff), because they've been there from the beginning. I thank old friends (Mr. Hernandez, Ms. Jordan, Mrs. Navarette, Mrs. Quezada) and new (Mrs. Soto & her team, Mrs. Marissa & her fabulous math coaches; Mary Headly). I thank my friends down in South Arkansas (Mr. Tom, Mrs. Vines, Janice & the teaching community) and in Chicago, Mr. Heidencamp & Staff). I thank Terri, Scott and Elena for all their support. I thank God, for every day he gives me to do this work.

1

Creating a Community of Learners in a Math-Rich Classroom

Figure 1.1 Anchor Chart: In Our Classroom

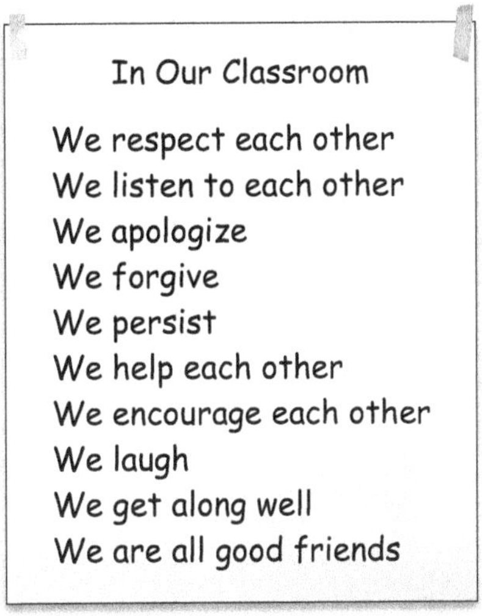

In Our Classroom

We respect each other
We listen to each other
We apologize
We forgive
We persist
We help each other
We encourage each other
We laugh
We get along well
We are all good friends

Math Workshop is about a group of children learning and working together throughout the year in a structured instructional format that has multiple spaces for individual, partner, and small-group work. Students collaborate and learn about math in a space that is invigorating, rigorous, and standards based. They look forward to working on projects, playing games, and spending quality time with their teacher. Math Workshop is meant to be part of what memories are made of. So how do you create such a space? Day by day, week by week, throughout the year, your goal is to develop students' "productive mathematical behaviors, model mathematical thinking and foster a productive disposition" (Hunter & Anthony, 2011).

Mathematical behaviors are how people act as mathematicians. Mathematical thinking is how people engage their minds with mathematical concepts and talk about and show what they know. A productive disposition is how people see themselves as mathematicians and how motivated they are to engage with the mathematics based on their beliefs about how well they can do the math. A productive disposition includes "confidence, flexibility, perseverance, interest, creativity, appreciation, reflection and monitoring" (Merz, 2009). The first few weeks are crucial in setting the "feeling tone" (to use a Madeline Hunter phrase) for the entire year.

Week 1: Beginning the Journey

The first week is about establishing Math Workshop as a structure for teaching and learning math (see Figure 1.5). During this week, you will introduce Math Workshop in general, and then the ways of being and doing as mathematicians framed around the National Council of Teachers of Mathematics (NCTM) Mathematical Processes (2000) and the Mathematical Practices (2010). It is important to work on building a mathematical community of learners. You want your students to love learning, to love math, and to respect each other. This comes about in an intentional way, when you set out to create a community of respectful learners.

Figure 1.2 Anchor Chart: Community

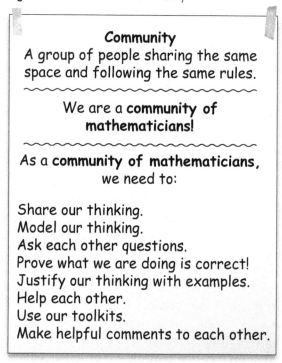

Community
A group of people sharing the same space and following the same rules.

We are a **community of mathematicians!**

As a **community of mathematicians,** we need to:

Share our thinking.
Model our thinking.
Ask each other questions.
Prove what we are doing is correct!
Justify our thinking with examples.
Help each other.
Use our toolkits.
Make helpful comments to each other.

During this first week, you can use mini-lessons about community that are anchored by charts to help your students to learn and then remember how the community works. You should emphasize communication and participation. Set the tone that explanation, justification, and "friendly argumentation" is what you expect in your discussions (Goos, 2004; Hunter & Anthony, 2011).

Figure 1.3 Anchor Chart on Being Great Mathematicians

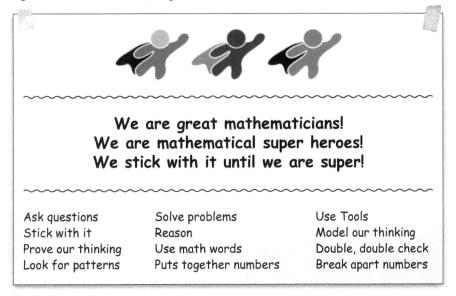

We are great mathematicians!
We are mathematical super heroes!
We stick with it until we are super!

Ask questions	Solve problems	Use Tools
Stick with it	Reason	Model our thinking
Prove our thinking	Use math words	Double, double check
Look for patterns	Puts together numbers	Break apart numbers

Figure 1.4 Anchor Chart: Manners Make a Difference

Manners Make a Difference

Will you please...?
May I please?
Excuse me...
I'm sorry for...
Can you help me...?
Will you wait a few minutes please?

Your students will learn that they will be working together respectfully to learn all the math they need to learn this year. You should have a general introduction of the math—an overview of the big math goals for the year. You should emphasize learning about talking to each other about math and learning with each other. See Figures 1.1, 1.2, 1.3, 1.4, 1.5, and 1.6 for sample anchor charts that can help you set the general tone.

Figure 1.5 Anchor Chart: Our Class Promise

Our Class Promise

We promise to work together.
We promise to help each other.
We promise to stick with it until
we get it.
We promise to get along.
We promise to do our best so
we can have a great school year!

Susie Jon Claire Maria
Roger Mary David Raul

Figure 1.6 Anchor Chart: Math Workshop

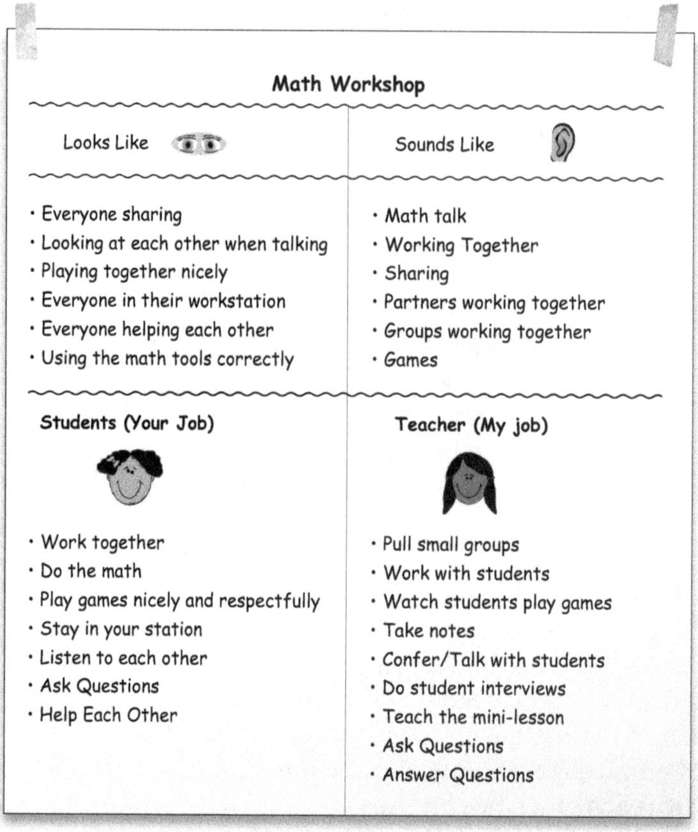

Math Workshop

Looks Like	Sounds Like
• Everyone sharing	• Math talk
• Looking at each other when talking	• Working Together
• Playing together nicely	• Sharing
• Everyone in their workstation	• Partners working together
• Everyone helping each other	• Groups working together
• Using the math tools correctly	• Games

Students (Your Job)	Teacher (My job)
• Work together	• Pull small groups
• Do the math	• Work with students
• Play games nicely and respectfully	• Watch students play games
• Stay in your station	• Take notes
• Listen to each other	• Confer/Talk with students
• Ask Questions	• Do student interviews
• Help Each Other	• Teach the mini-lesson
	• Ask Questions
	• Answer Questions

Week 2: Learning to Persevere, Reason, and Talk Mathematics

Devote the second week to learning more about persevering as a mathematician (a concept as important as stamina is to reading). For example, introduce your students to problem solving. They will learn about persevering through a problem, modeling their thinking, and then explaining what they did. You should scaffold student thinking through problems with templates. You can have a class template for the problem of the day and individual templates for work in stations. Templates help students to organize themselves and address all aspects of problem solving. See the word problem template in Figure 1.7.

During this week, spend some time on the idea of perseverance. This is one of the greatest gifts you can teach your students. They need to learn that they have to "stick with it" and "wrestle" with a problem. You need to teach this explicitly through what Dweck (2006) calls a "growth curriculum." This is in reference to an explicit curriculum that teaches children to stick with it until they get it. You can create your own growth curriculum by having posters up and routines that talk about students' perseverance in math.

Figure 1.7 Problem Solving Template

Name: **Date:**	
Visualize and summarize	Make a plan
Solve one way	Check another
Write an equation	
Explain your thinking	

(Newton, 2014)

Figure 1.8 Building a Growth Mindset

	Whatever I think is true! If I think I can, I can. If I think I can't, I can't. The power is in my thoughts!			

		Fixed Mindset	*Growth Mindset*
"I've missed more than 9000 shots in my career. I've lost almost 300 games. 26 times, I've been trusted to take the game winning shot and missed. I've failed over and over and over again in my life. And that is why I succeed." Michael Jordan **So, what are you going to do when you don't get it right the first time?** *Watch video: https://www.pinterest.com /pin/142004194476404925	*Your brain grows the more you learn!*	I can't do it. I don't try very hard. I get mad. I give up.	I can do it. I keep trying until I get it. I stick with it. I know I'll get it.
Great mathematicians make many mistakes! They are proof that we are trying!	***The Power of Yet!*** I don't get it yet! But I will! *Show the video https://www.pinterest.com/ pin/142004194476405233/	**Mindset Matters!**	

(Newton, 2014)

Start this discussion at the beginning of the year and continue it throughout the school year, having daily and weekly routines (see Figure 1.8). (Be sure to see my Pinterest board about growth mindset at www.pinterest.com/ pin/142004194476404925/)

In your teaching environment, hang posters like the one in Figure 1.8 showing Michael Jordan's famous quote.

Next, introduce your students to reasoning. They can discuss solving different types of problems of the week. One type of problem is where your students will go from words to numbers (to decontextualize), and the other type is where they will go from numbers to words (to contextualize); see Figure 1.9. This idea of getting students to become problem posers as well as problem solvers has been around for a while; however, it has gained even more recognition in the last few years (CCSS, 2010).

Help your students begin to practice routines such as *Prove It, Convince Me,* and *True or False?* These are all reasoning routines where students

Figure 1.9 We pose and solve word problems!

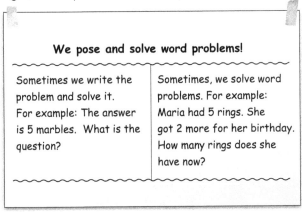

We pose and solve word problems!

Sometimes we write the problem and solve it. For example: The answer is 5 marbles. What is the question?	Sometimes, we solve word problems. For example: Maria had 5 rings. She got 2 more for her birthday. How many rings does she have now?

Figure 1.10 We reason in this class!

We reason in this class!

We ask:	We say:
Does that make since? Can you prove it? Are you sure? Is there another way?	Convince me that you are right! I agree with you because… I disagree with you because… We need to double check… I got a different answer…

have to prove their thinking, convince others that their argument makes sense, and decide whether a given problem or equation is true or false (see Figure 1.10).

During this time, introduce your students to the "5 talk moves" (Chapin, O'Connor & Anderson, 2003); see Figure 1.11. Chapin and colleagues describe these strategies for facilitating a discussion as:

> "talk moves" that support mathematical thinking, talk formats that provide different ways to organize students for conversations and ideas for creating a classroom where respect and equal access to participation are valued norms.
>
> (Chapin, O'Connor & Anderson, 2003, p. 11)

When you directly teach your students how to engage in discussion with each other, you set up a framework for success. You can make a classroom poster, talk about it with your students, and then practice the talk moves.

Figure 1.11 Five Talk Moves

5 Talk Moves (Way we talk in a discussion)				
Repeating	**Revoicing/ Restate**	**Reasoning**	**Adding On**	**Wait Time**
It is when you say what the person said.	It is to check that we all heard and understood.	It is when you think about whether you agree or disagree.	It is when you want to add something to what has been said.	It is when you give someone time to think.
It sounds like: "You said that . . . ." "Can you say it again?" "Can you repeat it?"	It sounds like: "Who can repeat what was just said?" "Who can say that in their own words?"	It sounds like: "Who agrees and who disagrees and why?" "I agree" or "I disagree."	It sounds like: "Who wants to add to that . . . .?" "I want to add that . . . ." "That makes me think . . . ." "Tell us more . . . ." "Who wants to say more about that . . . .?"	It sounds like: "Think about that before you speak . . . ." "I need a few minutes to think . . . ." Just silence (everybody thinking).
Chapin notes that "deep thinking and powerful reasoning do not always correlate with clear verbal expression. . . . Revoicing can make one student's idea available to others, give them time to hear it again. . . . Revoicing provides more 'thinking space' and can help all students track what is going on mathematically" (Chapin, O'Connor & Anderson, 2003, pp. 10, 13).	Chapin notes that this "gives the rest of the class another rendition" of what is being discussed and gives "more time to process" what has been said.		Chapin notes that this allows everyone to "weigh in" on what is being discussed.	

Figure 1.12 More Talk Moves

Inviting Student Participation	Probing Students' Thinking	Creating Opportunities to Engage with Another's Reasoning
It is a polling of the class to get the collective thoughts.	It is digging deeper into student thought.	It is requiring students to engage with each other's thinking.
It sounds like: "Let's hear what everybody else used as a model."	It sounds like: "Can you tell us a little bit more using numbers, words, and/or pictures how you thought about $1/2 \times 4$?"	It sounds like: "So what I want you to do now is solve 12×15 using Ted's strategy."

Herbel-Eisenmann, Steele, and Cirillo (cited in Cirillo, 2013) built on the talk moves of Chapin et al. (2003) and came up with what they call "teacher discourse moves" as a tool to facilitate productive classroom discussions. Figure 1.12 shows the three new twists they added to talk moves.

Kristin Edwards (www.pinterest.com/pin/19351473372809858/) has a great idea to get students talking. She puts accountable talk stems on Popsicle sticks. There are many ways you can use these talk stems to jumpstart a conversation. You can include them in everyone's toolkit or you can pass them out during a conversation with the whole class. Students can use them when working with partners or in groups. They provide a visual written language prompt (see Figure 1.13).

Several other teachers have made math talk rings by putting talk stems on a rectangle and attaching it to a ring. This is a great idea. Your students should actually write the talk stems out on index cards so that they truly own the questions, and then put them on rings and keep them in their toolkits.

You should also have a talk ring divided up into different types of questions by color so that the questions stay fresh as well. You should think of their role in orchestrating the talk in the classroom. This is done with specific teacher "talk moves." Not only do you have to have a

Figure 1.13 Talk Stems on Popsicle Sticks

Can you solve it another way?

Can you prove it?

I agree

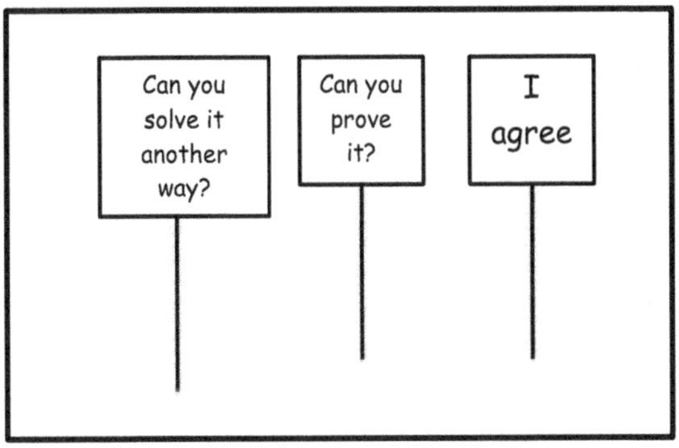

repertoire of great questions, but you should also have specific ways of facilitating the discussion using the above-mentioned talk moves. You support math talk by posting anchor charts that your students can refer to, as well as by doing weekly reflections in the older grades (see Figures 1.14, 1.15, and 1.16).

Figure 1.14 Anchor Chart: Math Talk Stems

Math Talk Stems:

When talking about your thinking:

I'm thinking…
I'm wondering if…
I'm seeing…
It reminds me of…
I'm feeling like…
I'm noticing…
I've decided…
I learned that…
I was confused when…

Figure 1.15 Anchor Chart: Great Math Questions to Ask Each Other!

Great Math Questions to Ask Each Other!

Are you sure?
Can you prove it?
How do you know?
Convince me that…
What's another way?
Show me how you know?
What is your strategy?
Would you model that for me?
Can you explain that?

Figure 1.16 Weekly Reflection Tool

Name: Talk is important in math class. This week during our discussions this is how I did.			
	Great	**Good**	**Working on it!**
I thought about and answered questions.			
I asked my classmates questions.			
Explained my thinking.			
Modeled my thinking.			
Agreed/Disagreed with someone else's thinking.			
I challenged someone else's thinking.			
I added on to someone else's thinking/I piggybacked.			
Overall I would say that my math talk is.....			

Based on Chapin, O'Connor & Anderson (2003); adapted from Ronan (2010) www. lowell.k12.ma.us/files/_laCKB_/9227f001745644ea3745a49013852ec4/My_Math_ Talk_Moves.pdf

Where Do Good Questions Come From?

Good questions are a linchpin of productive classroom discussion (see Figure 1.17). One way to get your students to be able to ask and answer good questions is to start the year by having a question of the week. Each week, ask a different question and have your students work on that answer until

Figure 1.17 Great Websites with Great Questions

Here is a list of great websites with great questions:

http://mrsshannonsclass.weebly.com/uploads/5/6/7/8/5678537/mathematics_questions.pdf

www-tc.pbs.org/teachers/_files/pdf/TL_MathCard.pdf

http://hannatli.weebly.com/uploads/1/8/8/3/18838262/dok_chart_and_stems.pdf

www.carrollk12.org/instruction/instruction/elementary/math/curriculum/common/ (see question starters)

they get good at it. For example, a question of the week could be: "Is there another way?" You can ask this question in whole-group and small-group discussions, your students can ask this question when they turn and talk with their partners and the groups can focus on this question during group work. By the end of the week, your students will have a pretty good grasp of this question. It now is part of their repertoire. The next week, you can ask a different question. You can start the school year off with these four important questions:

> Question 1: Can you prove it?
> Question 2: Is there another way?
> Question 3: Are you sure about that? How do you know?
> Question 4: Do you agree or disagree?

Week 3: Showing What You Know and Double Checking It!

You should devote a few days to talking about modeling thinking and using tools. Your students should understand that they can model their thinking through drawings, manipulatives, acting out, and diagramming. You should review what has been taught in previous years and then introduce new models as appropriate throughout the year. From this initial conversation, your students should take away the idea that great mathematicians model their thinking. This is a good time to remind your students of the difference between making Picasso masterpieces and doing quick mathematical sketches. You should practice doing this so your students don't spend 15 minutes drawing a marble.

Introducing Tools and Toolkits

On the day that tools are discussed, introduce your students to the idea of class toolkits. They should do a few activities to familiarize themselves with the classroom tools. In the beginning of the year, the students are revisiting tools they used last year and talking about ways to use those tools. Throughout the year, as you introduce tools, you can explain how to use them in specific contexts. Thus, toolkits are added to throughout the year.

Remember that the teaching environment is also part of your toolkit, so you should introduce your students to and work with life-sized classroom tools such as ten frames, number lines, and fraction bars. It is very important for you to have tools in your meeting area from the beginning. Tools are what your students use to think (see Figures 1.18 and 1.19). They should have tools in the area where they are sitting. There are two parts to a toolkit: The first part is the actual items, like the counting cubes, 1-inch tiles, decimal squares, base-ten blocks, ten frames, and number lines; the second part is the templates, like geoboard paper, pattern block paper, hundreds grids, and decimal grids.

Discussing Precision

Finally, you should spend some time on precision—both in calculations and language (CCSS, 2010). The idea that students should use precise language and double-check their work for accuracy is discussed in both the Common Core Mathematical Practices (CCSS, 2010) and the NCTM process standards (NCTM, 2000). You should introduce your students to various routines of how math is a language that they will be learning and using all year long. Your students must use precise mathematical vocabulary. From the very first week of school, your students should play math vocabulary games at least once a week, because math is a language; and if your students don't know

Figure 1.18 Using Tools in the Meeting Areas

Rules for Tools!	Tools
We use tools to help us think! We keep our toolkits organized. We use them when we need them. We put them up when we are done. We use our templates to sketch out answers.	We use many different tools, Bears and counters, cubes They're cool! We know how to use them well, And clean up when we hear the bell!

Newton 2014

Figure 1.19 Math Toolkits

Primary Toolkits (K–2)	Upper Elementary Toolkits (Grades 3–5)
Materials:	**Materials:**
• Unifix Cubes • Fraction Squares, Circles Bars • Pattern Blocks • Bears • Base-Ten Blocks • 1-inch Tiles • Dice; Double Dice • Triple Dice; Dotted Dice • Mini-dominos • Mini Flash Cards • Numeral Dice • 2 Colored Counters • Clear Bingo Chips • Rekenrek • Ruler • Calculator • Coins	• Unifix Cubes • Fraction Squares, Circles Bars • Pattern Blocks • Bears (for fraction set models; also for multiplication models) • Base-Ten Blocks • Elapsed Time Ruler • 1-inch Tiles • Decimal Squares • Decimal Wheels • Dice; Double Dice; Triple Dice • Mini Dominos • Mini Flash Cards • 2 Colored Counters • Clear Bingo Chips • Ruler • Protractor • Calculator • Coins • Pattern Blocks
Templates:	**Templates:**
• *Five Frame* • *Ten Frame* • *Double Ten Frame* • *100 chart* • *120 chart* • *200 chart* • *Number Lines* • *Number Ladders* • *Number Tracks* • *Unifix Cubes Paper* • *Fraction Squares, Circles, Bars* • *Pattern Block Paper* • *Base-Ten Grid Paper* • *Geoboard Paper*	• *Unifix Cubes Paper (use for fractions and multiplication groups of problems)* • *Fraction Squares, Circles, Bars* • *Fraction Number Lines* • *Pattern Block Paper* • *Base-Ten Grid Paper* • *Ten Thousand Grid Paper* • *Cm Grid Paper* • *Inch Grid Paper* • *Decimal Wheels* • *Geoboard Paper*
Tools depend on the grade. These are general suggestions for the given grade bands.	

Newton 2014

the words, then they can't speak the language. Play games such as whole-class charades, guess the word, tic-tac-toe, and bingo so your students have a chance to practice the relevant vocabulary words. In the beginning of the year, be sure to practice the words from the year before.

Figure 1.20 Teaching the Double Double Check

Did you **double double** check?	
Did you check the math?	Did you check the answer? Does it answer the question? Does it make sense?

Newton 2014

Your other focus should be accuracy. Your students should learn about the importance of double checking (see Figure 1.3 for a great example of introducing the word "double checking"). I teach the students to "double double check!" They must check the math and check that the answer matches the question (see Figure 1.20).

Price writes about using a particular phraseology to get students to double check without feeling bad about getting the answer wrong (Price, 2003). Price writes about a teacher who uses the strategy of saying "nearly" when she wants students to look again. She will say that something is *"nearly"* correct, which prompts the students to recognize that they made a mistake, correct it, and then have the confidence to talk about it:

> Debbie and the children are building a class ethos where it is **OK to "have a go"** and to make mistakes. The ethos has a positive effect on the children's attitudes and motivation in mathematics. As a result the children are wanting to become more able learners of mathematics, to attain mastery of the domain.
>
> (Price, 2003, p. 7)

Week 4: Introducing Math Workstations and the Guided Math Groups

Your rollout of the general structure and the ways of being and doing as mathematicians will take about two to three weeks, depending on your grade and the particular group of students. After doing a few weeks of Math Workshop orientation, community building, and working on the ways of being and doing as a mathematician, you should roll out Math Workstations. Your students will learn how to get out the workstations, do the math, and then put them away. They will learn how to work alone, with partners, and in small groups. In the beginning, your students should practice using workstations with concepts from the priority standards of the year before. When introducing the stations, play the games with your whole class, and then differentiate them. Teach some games to a small group only. Spend the time needed so your students know exactly what to do during Math Workstations. *Do not start small groups until all your students understand what they are doing.*

Introducing Small Guided Math Groups

After your students learn how to work with the Math Workstations, form them into small guided math groups. Start small. For the first few days, pull only one group. Add the number of groups that you pull as the class gets accustomed to working on their own. During this week, your students practice coming to small groups and learn the architecture of the small-group lessons. They participate in the introduction, the student activities—playing games and doing math—and then the summarization of the meeting. They then transition into their workstation, or if it is the last rotation of the day, they go to the meeting area for the Share.

Practicing the Workshop

After you have rolled out everything, spend about a week on practicing the workshop and the debriefing session at the end of the workshop. All of this takes time, but it is well worth the invested effort. You want to spend time considering the entire workshop and discuss with your students what is going really well and what needs improvement. Your students (depending on the grade) should have to talk and write about what went well and what needs work. This reflection period before your class goes into full workshop mode is absolutely necessary. This lays a firm foundation for the upcoming year. This investment will pay off, and if it is rushed, it will show throughout the year. It is a good idea to reflect on the *ins and outs* of Math Workshop at least once a month throughout the year.

Classroom Norms Versus Classroom Math Norms
In building a classroom of curious, confident, public mathematicians, you naturally infuse the social norms of the everyday classroom. However, there is some interesting research by Yackel and Cobb (1996) that distinguishes between regular social norms and sociomathematical norms. Sociomathematical norms take the thinking directly to the math. It's the idea that yes, mathematicians do share common ground with other disciplines, but there are some ways of being and doing in math that are specific to math. I think the distinction is worth considering a bit more here (see Figure 1.21).

Summary

Building a community of learners takes time. It is much more intensive than a traditional math classroom (see Figure 1.22). It is well worth the investment at the beginning of the year so that your students can thrive throughout the year. Your students must learn the importance of persevering through problem solving. They have to learn how to communicate

Figure 1.21 Social Norms Versus Sociomathematical Norms

Social Norms	Sociomathematical Norms
Questioning is part of the culture: The teacher and the students question each other's thinking	The teacher and students ask each other questions that press for mathematical reasoning, including proving, justifying, defending, elaborating, clarifying and challenging: **Ask questions that clarify an explanation** (What did you mean by? What did you do in that [part]? Can you show us what you mean . . .? Can you draw a picture of what you are thinking? Can you use the model to show that?) **Ask questions that lead to justification** (How do you know it works: Can you convince us? Why would that tell you to? Why does that work like that? Are you sure that . . .? So what happens if . . . What about if you say . . . does that still work?) **Ask questions that lead to generalizations** (Does it always work? Can you make connections between . . .? Can you see any patterns? Can you make connections between . . .? How is this the same or different to what we did before? Would that work with all numbers?) (Hunter & Anthony, 2011, pp. 3–4)
Students explain what they are thinking	Students have to explain their solutions using math words, strategies and models. They have to provide a "mathematical reason or justification for their thinking rather than just a description of their thinking" (Hunter & Anthony, 2011, pp. 3–4). Students justify their thinking with math language such as "I *know* that 2 of 3/4 is 1 1/2 *because* 3/4 + 1/4 is 1 whole and then we have 1/2 left. So, 3/4 + 3/4 = 1 1/2. The students are expected to use words like "so," "if," "then," and "because" to justify their thinking. Students are expected to agree or disagree with an argument.
Students work together to solve problems	Students are required to not only get a solution, but to think about the different ways to approach a problem mathematically and compare those ways, given the numbers.
Students solve problems using a variety of approaches	Students think about the efficiency of approaches and the various models to show their thinking. They are expected to "revise, extend and elaborate on sections others might not understand . . . predict questions that might be asked and prepare responses . . . work together to check, explain, re-explain" (Hunter & Anthony, 2011, p. 3). Students must explain how they did something, why it is correct and how to look at it in different ways.
Students see mistakes as part of learning	Students unpack their mistakes, look at them deeply and see how their mistakes help them to learn math.

Based on Yackel & Cobb (1996); adapted from Baxter (2010). http://emast.uoregon.edu/files/2011/01/ Social-and-Sociomathematical-Norms.pdf

Figure 1.22 Traditional Classroom vs. Math Workshop Classroom

Traditional Classroom	Math Workshop Classroom
Whole class (everybody hears the same things and then is expected to do work based on that; students listen and watch the teacher talk and do the math)	Whole class (everybody hears the same general mini-lesson; students go to small guided groups for follow-up)
Quiet individual seatwork (after watching the teacher, the students go to their desks and work alone to practice the textbook pages)	Individual work done in workstations (alone, with partners, and in small groups)
Teacher talks/students listen	Everybody talks, the teacher encourages students to comment on the mathematical thinking of others (child to child talk; teacher to child talk; child to teacher to child talk)
Direct instruction	Varied teaching formats: direct instruction, videos, interactive lectures, discussion, small groups
Text book dominated	Text is one of many resources; texts could even be main resource, but other supplementary resources are pulled in to address the different needs, learning styles, and interests of all the students; some schools use teacher-created curricula rather than a standard textbook
Very little guided practice and checking for understanding	A big emphasis is put on guided practice and checking for understanding throughout the teaching of the unit
Emphasis is on individual work; Learning mathematics is seen as an individual endeavor	Emphasis is on collaborative learning; learning mathematics is seen as a social and collaborative activity anchored in continuous communication
Traditional teacher question–student response cycle	Everybody asks questions and everybody responds; the discussion is about conjecturing, proving, clarifying, refuting, agreeing, disagreeing, reasoning, generalizing. There are "communication and participation" frameworks that structure meaningful student engagement in rich mathematical discussions (Hunter & Anthony, 2011).

Figure 1.22 (Continued)

Teacher is the only evaluator	Teacher and students participate in the evaluation process through rubrics, checklists, interactive journals, conferences, reflection sheets, weekly check-ins; emphasis is on self-monitoring and self-checking; also, students engage in peer-monitoring and peer-checking
Focus is on getting the chapter done . . . page by page; fidelity to program only	Focus is on sense-making, differentiation, student-driven, standards-oriented fidelity to the developmental process of learning math

Newton 2014

with each other using math words. They need time to speak, listen, process, record, and learn. They need to learn how to model their thinking and show what they are talking about by using the tools appropriate to their grade. They also need to learn to "double, double check" their thinking and their work. Both national standards (CCSS, 2010) and state standards are promoting these processes and practices so that students know math deeply, and own it. A community of mathematical learners expects to have to explain, listen, question, justify, verify, expand upon, critique, model, defend, and show what they know. In order to scaffold this type of environment, you should use talk structures and language stems that promote listening intensely to the conversation at hand. The norm in your class should promote "intellectual risk taking" so that your students develop "mathematical argumentation, intellectual autonomy and mathematical power" (Hunter & Anthony, 2011).

Key Points

- Great mathematicians live in a respectful community
- Great mathematicians work together throughout workshop
- Great mathematicians persevere in problem solving
- Great mathematicians share their thinking and use math words
- Great mathematicians listen to each other and question each other
- Great mathematicians use tools
- Great mathematicians model their thinking and double check their work
- There is a difference between regular classroom norms and socio-mathematical norms.

Reflection Questions

1. How much time do you spend in the beginning of the year developing a community of thoughtful, motivated, determined mathematicians?
2. Do you have toolkits? Do students use them every day? Is your classroom a toolkit? Is there stuff readily available for students to explain their thinking? What can you improve?
3. What routines do you have for vocabulary? How do you know that your students really know and own the math vocabulary? What *evidence* do you have?
4. What is the first thing you will use from this chapter and why?

2

Living and Learning in a Mathematically Rich Space

A glance around the room tells how important math is . . .

Dr. Nicki Newton

The Environment

Children spend a little less than half of their waking day in school. Essentially, the classroom is one of the places they live and learn. They make sense of their world, form values, and become who they will be later, all in school classrooms. Many classrooms that I walk into are literacy-rich environments, "dripping with literacy" to use an old buzz phrase. Yet, many times I see very few drops of math.

All teachers must do a better job at making math important and relevant. Our students must come to realize that our lives are mathematical. From the time we wake up, literally until the time we go to bed, our lives involve some math. This math goes far beyond the schoolbook version, which rarely focuses on "real daily lived math."

You should stress upfront the importance of math by having an environment that supports mathematical thinking. Where is your general meeting area? Your general meeting area is a place where you and the students meet to discuss, explain, and model thinking. Do you have math tools so that your students can use the tools when they are doing math? I find that many times the tools are on the walls, serving for nothing more than great wall paper. You don't hang your hammer on your wall—so why would you hang tools that you need on the wall? Yes, you should have number lines up . . . but you should also have number lines and number ladders available for students to hold, touch, and use when they need them (the same goes for number grids and multiplication tables). Some people even use mini-offices (this is where the students use a file folder to paste different tools on all sides, such as number grids, number lines, number words, etc.) to provide instant access to resources that students need. Sometimes there is a pocket where students can store flashcards. The environment that you create either fosters or hinders your students' mathematical development. The physical space is very important. What do your walls say about the importance of math in your class?

Gathering Spaces

Whole-Group Meeting Area

You should designate a whole-group meeting area. In this area you need general resources. You need your pointers, your various tools, your easel and chart paper, your markers, and your sticky notes. The general meeting area is a place to open the Math Workshop and close it. Also, sometimes you hold seminars (a short talk about something of importance) here on free-choice days. It is important that you have big tools in or near this area, such as big five, ten, or double ten frames, so your students can act out problems, a number line that they can walk on, and a big number bracelet (in the primary grades). You should also have a relevant number grid in this area. In primary grades, it would be a number grid to 100 or 120. In the upper elementary grades, it could be to 200, and for some grades, a decimal number grid. Furthermore, you should have a number line on a sentence strip so your students can come up and touch it. Depending on the grade, the number line should be whole numbers, fractions, or decimals. Remember that if it is fractions or decimals, it should have pictures. Basically, in the whole-group meeting area, you should have big versions of much of the stuff that is in your students' toolkits.

Workstations

The desks clustered together are where your students will meet in their Math Workstations. Most of the physical stations will be in baskets, buckets, or bins. Some, however—such as the computer station, the SMART Board station, or the math big book station—will be in their respective places. In terms of desks, some teachers have made their student desks and their kidney tables into white board spaces. This is very interesting indeed. This provides for some different possibilities while working with students. Seating arrangements and workspaces should foster opportunities for your students to move around the room freely and comfortably. They should also allow for maximum collaboration.

Conference Table

The Guided Math table is a general place to meet your small groups. But remember that guided math groups can happen in a variety of places. You can meet your students in the computer station, at the rug, in a workstation, or at the kidney table. The focus isn't the place, it's the math.

General Mathematical Environment

Daily Schedule

Daily schedules help students to organize their time. It is important to have a general daily schedule (preferably with analog clock pictures) alongside the time and the activity. It is also suggested that you have picture clues, especially in primary classrooms, special education classrooms, and classrooms with English language learners who might not have access to the text. A schedule allows your students to make real-world connections with time and also provides a real context for telling elapsed time. You should also display a detailed schedule of Math Workshop so your students can learn and keep track of the flow of the workshop (see Figures 2.1 and 2.2).

Figure 2.1 Math Workshop Wheel

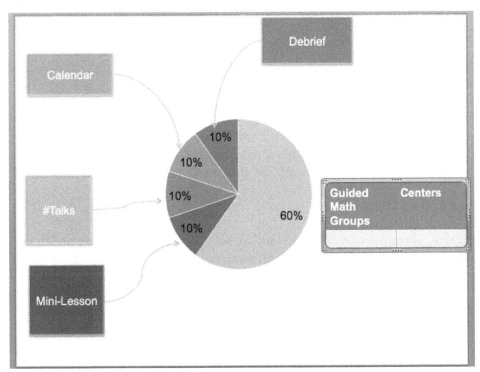

Figure 2.2 Math Workshop Schedule

Math Workshop
9:15–9:35 **Opening:** Energizers Fluency Routines Number Talks Problem of the Day Mini-Lesson
9:35–10:05 **Student Work Period:** Guided Math Groups Math Workstations Conferences/Interviews Seminars
10:05–10:15 **Debrief:** Reflections Congratulations Share Chair Journaling

Class Clocks

It is really important to landmark your clocks. The landmarks depend on the grade. Kindergarten clocks should be marked as o'clock. First grade should have clocks marked by o'clock and half past. Second grade should have clocks marked by 5-minute increments and the language o'clock, half past, quarter to. Third grade and up should be highly scaffolded with clocks that have the numbers and the words as well. Some teachers put nickels or hands around the clock to reinforce counting by 5s.

Math Word Walls

Math is a language. If your students don't know the words, then they can't speak the language. Math word walls should help to teach the children the words. There are a variety of ways to do this and a tremendous number of free resources. I find that many people have word walls up just to decorate the room with some math stuff. The students don't really ever own those words. You want to put up a word wall that teaches. Your word walls should be illustrated. They should also be kept in workstations so that they live throughout the school year. Only the words from the current unit of study should be up. Sometimes, teachers will have two lists. One list has high-frequency words that stay up all year, and a second list has the current words for the chapter. A few examples are shown in Figures 2.3, 2.4, 2.5, 2.6, 2.7, and 2.8.

Figure 2.3 Metric System Units

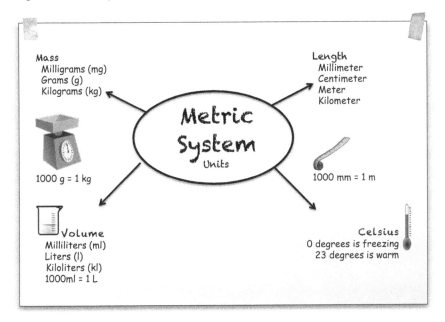

Figure 2.4 Fraction Word Wall

Fraction Word Wall		
Parts of fractions	**Types of fractions**	**Fraction Operations**
Numerator 2/3 (top number)	Unit Fractions/common fraction/proper fractions 1/2,1/5 (fractions smaller than 1)	Adding: 1/2+1/2 = 1
Denominator 2/3 (bottom number)	Improper fractions 4/2, 5/3 (fractions greater than 1)	Subtracting 1/2–1/4 = 1/4
Vinculum 3/4 (fraction bar)	Benchmark fractions 1/2,1/4,3/4 (fractions we use every day)	Multiplying 4x1/2 = 2
Fractions (any part of a whole) 3/4, 5/6	Mixed Number 1 1/2, 2 3/4 (a mixed number is a whole number and a fraction)	Simplifying 6/12 = 1/2

Clip art created by Jason's Online Classroom (www.teacherspayteachers.com/store/Jasons-Online-Classroom). Copyright 2012 Jason Perez. Used with permission.

Figure 2.5 Math Word Wall

Math Word Wall	
Words we use all the time: **Explain** – Tell in detail (step by step) **Justify/Prove** – To give examples using numbers, words and pictures **Defend** – To say why you think what you think **Challenge** – To say why you think something is not correct; to say why you disagree with something **Model** – To show your thinking with drawings, diagrams, objects and/or numbers **Use a visual image** – Show with pictures/drawings/sketches **Verify** – Double check	**Words we are learning:** **Fractions** – A fraction is a part of a whole 1/2, 1/4, 5/6 **Equivalent fractions** – Fractions that equal the same amount 3/4 = 6/8 **Numerator** – 2/4 (top number) (shows how many parts of the whole we are talking about) **Denominator** – 2/4 (bottom number) (shows how many parts the whole has been divided into)

Clip art created by Jason's Online Classroom (www.teacherspayteachers.com/store/Jasons-Online-Classroom). © 2012 Jason Perez. Used with permission.

Figure 2.6 Our Math Words

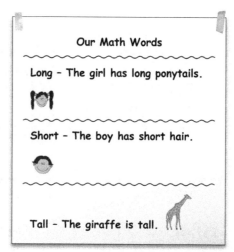

Stock image of giraffe from Dollar Photo Club, www. dollarphotoclub.com/Search?k=sea&filters%5Bcontent_ type%3Aphoto%5D=1&filters%5Bcontent_type% 3Aillustration%5D=1&filters%5Bcontent_type% 3Avector%5D=1&search=Search

Figure 2.7 Math Words Format

Mrs. Clancy uses a particular format
for introducing math words in her
kindergarten class:

Our new word is . . .
Plus sign
We can draw it . . .
*(Pictures with post-its drawn by
the kids)*
It means . . .
*Putting things together. We use it when
we are adding stuff.*

*Source: http://kckindergartentimes.blogspot.com/
search?updated-max=2011–11–19T07:00:00–08:
00&max-results=12*

Figure 2.8 Word Box: Multiplication Sign

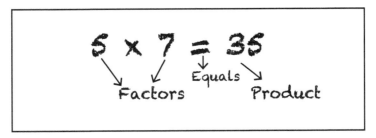

There are many ways to set up word walls. You can do them as language experience opportunities. A great structure for this is the Frayer Model whereby students discuss the definition, an example, a non-example, and a real-life connection (Figure 2.9). See Figure 2.10 for more examples of math word walls.

Another great way to put up vocabulary in your classroom is to decorate the doors, windows, cabinets, floor, and any other spaces with the vocabulary. So, for example, on the door you would write "horizontal" above it and "vertical" on the side. You might write "parallel" and "perpendicular" on the opposite sides of the windows to show parallel and then perpendicular lines. At the front of the class you might have a right hand on the right side of the room and a left hand on the left side of the room.

Figure 2.9 Word Box: Plus Sign

Word Box Plus Sign	
The class definition: It is a sign that we use to show how to put things together. We use it when we are adding numbers. +	**A real world use:** Maria: Like when we add apples Tom: Like when we add money Sue: We could add teddy bears
An illustration 🍎🍎.🍎🍎 2 + 2 = 4	**What it is not** **Subtraction** **It's not take away.** 🍎🍎🍎🍎

Figure 2.10 Sources for Math Vocabulary

Some great places to get math vocabulary
Posters: www.greatmathsgames.com/division/item/66-quotient.html
Done word walls: www.graniteschools.org/mathvocabulary/ www.doe.virginia.gov/instruction/mathematics/resources/vocab_cards/
Examples: www.pinterest.com/drnicki7/mathematical-practice-6-precision/

Math Manipulatives/Toolkits

Students should also have their own toolkits. Some teachers make communal toolkits that stay in a centralized location, and students get them as they need them. Other teachers allow their students to keep their toolkits in their desks, cubbies, or chair pockets. Still other teachers set up group toolkits. There are several ways to do it. Choose one that works for you. However, whatever you do, make sure that your students can access their toolkit whenever and wherever they need it.

Student Math Thinking Notebook/Class Notebook

It is important that your students have their own "Thinking Notebook." I refer to it specifically as a Thinking Notebook because I want students to realize that when we go into this notebook, we are writing down ideas based on thought. When we open it up, it should signify that we are about to do some deep work. The Thinking Notebook should be organized so that students can go to the pages they need when they need them. The number of parts the notebook has will depend on the grade level. At the minimum, your students should have a part for routines and a part for word problems. In the upper grades, your students should have a part for math vocabulary and reflections. You should also have a big class notebook for daily reflections, class Write Alouds, and general notes and thoughts (see Figure 2.11). Daily reflections are done during the Share (see Chapter 8). You should do class Write Alouds often; you can use them to model different types of writing in math. General notes and thoughts are a space where you and the students can record "aha" moments that may occur during the Math Workshop that they want to be sure to write down somewhere and discuss later.

Figure 2.11 Class Journal

11/14/2014
Today in math class we worked on addition. We spent time in workstations and small guided math groups. In small guided math groups we were adding with different models. In our workstations we worked on adding doubles with unifix cubes, playing a doubles game at the computer and playing a doubles card game and a doubles board game. We are studying doubles because it is a strategy for adding fast. Doubles are when you add a number to itself. Here are some examples:

2 + 2   4 + 4   5 + 5

Math Library

The Math Library is where all your math picture books will be kept. For every unit of study, there is a plethora of good math literature to choose from. The idea of using a math mentor text throughout various units of study only enriches the teaching of mathematics. You can design benchmark activities related to the book that your students can work on during the unit in a Math Workstation. One idea is to keep some of the activities that go along with that book and the book in the Math Library so your students can work on the concepts in that book and play games that reinforce those activities. It is also good to have some math poem activities. Using and keeping up math poems, chants, and songs will further reinforce math concepts.

Data and Folder Center

In your room you should have a space to put the data folders and the Math Workstation folders. The data folders can be folders or binders for individual students. They will have individual students' quizzes, chapter tests, midyear tests, and sample student work. The workstation folders that contain the workstation activity sheets of completed and in-progress work can also be stored here. In this area you can also have a Math Data wall to reflect current class data. There are various ways to do this. The data could reflect where your class is on learning the math vocabulary, the content, fluency for the grade, or something else. Math Data walls give a general overview of the status of your class. They should not show names, but they should display data in either a bar graph, line plot, or pictograph. Have your students set some specific goals and try to reach them. One idea is to have your students set specific goals and then track who is meeting their particular goals. This allows for differentiation but still holds everybody accountable.

Calendar Area

There are many things that you need in the calendar area to teach basic skills throughout the year. During your calendar time, you want your students to be able to be in charge of the activities (see Chapter 4 for more details).

Anchor Charts

It is important to have a variety of anchor charts throughout your classroom (see Figure 2.12). Most, if not all, anchor charts should be made with the children each year. Remember that your students will use anchor charts much more if they have been involved in creating them, because they will actually understand the charts and know how to use them and what to look for on them. Make it a habit to refer to the anchor charts frequently throughout the workshop so that your students view the charts as a helpful resource. Also be sure to take pictures of really essential charts and send them home so parents can see what your students are learning and how to do it for homework.

Some of the most effective charts that I have seen have used things other than just text. Brokofsky (https://jenniferbrokofsky.wordpress.com/2012/11/20/anchoring-the-learning-anchor-charts-in-math/) points out that "Pictures, graphic organizers, models, even manipulatives can be taped to the chart to support the concept. Just remember not to overload the chart. White space can make learning easier." Sometimes, you can start

Figure 2.12 Types of Math Anchor Charts

Type of Math Anchor Charts				
Strategy Charts	Procedure Charts	Content Charts	Social Skill Charts	Rules/Class Norms
What are 3 different ways to add 2-digit numbers?	How do we use a number line?	What does it mean to add something together?	How do we work with partners?	How do we use our tools?
What are 2 different ways to compare fractions?	How do we use decimal squares to add decimals?	What is a decimal?	What does it mean to respect each other?	How loud should we be in class?
Make charts big, visible, colorful, and legible.				

a chart and present it as a way to launch a mini-lesson, and then have your students fill it in. Oftentimes teachers will say that there is no room for the math anchor charts, and that they will get in trouble with the fire department if they put up more. Well, I always half-jokingly respond that "if we take down just a few of the literacy posters, we will have room for the math ones!" It's true. You should make sure that you have a balance of math and literacy posters up (besides the other content areas).

Anchor charts serve different purposes. Charts should focus on one mathematical skill, concept, or strategy at a time so that your students can get the information they need quickly. There are different types of posters that serve different functions. There are socialization posters about the community in general and how everyone should get along. Then there are math posters, both content and process. The content posters discuss the topic, and the process posters talk about models, strategies, and ways of thinking about a topic. To get even more specific, there are also strategy posters that emphasize different types of math strategies to use. You should have a mix of these posters in your classroom.

The strategy posters often stay up across units of study. Specific content posters can come down but should be stored in such a way that they are easily accessible to your students. Oftentimes teachers take pictures of the posters and send them home so parents can see what the students are learning in class. This makes it easier on everyone, because then the parents can see exactly what the students were doing in class. Many teachers also store these pictures in a photo album and flag them so that students can look at them whenever they need to. Some teachers store the anchor charts on plastic hangers (I would still advise flagging/tagging them) so that students can find the ones they are looking for when they need them.

Anchor Chart Storage

There are many ways to store anchor charts (see Figure 2.13). Your students should be able to reference them when they need to throughout the year (Leograndis, 2008). Also have your students make their own anchor chart notes. Some teachers have their students collect their anchor chart jottings into a "survival guide" that they keep all year long. These are great resources for students that reinforce strategies and concepts and put them right at the students' fingertips.

Figure 2.13 Ways to Store Anchor Charts

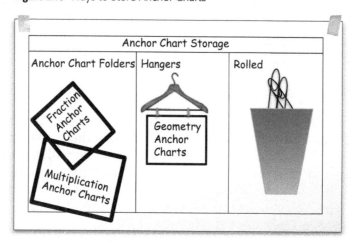

I Can Wall

There should be an *I can* wall in a section of your classroom that has all the *I can* statements for the current unit of study (see Figure 2.14). Have students focus on what they are learning to do and celebrate their continued growth. Dweck (2006) pushes us to think about the difference between "*I am* learning to" and "*I can*" because it has more room to reflect on progress. These statements should be illustrated. This is also a great place to have a status of the class. A Status of the Class chart has the *I can* statements written on the side and the student reflection statement written across the top. This is based on Marzano's idea of levels of understanding (Marzano, 2006). Some great examples of this in math can be found on the blog My Teacher Friend written by Brandi (http://myteacherfriend.blogspot.com/2012/10/math-benchmark-tracking.html), who expanded upon the idea and used it to show her students their data after a test (she uses names and numbers). Blogger Sarah K. (http://misskinbk.blogspot.com/2013/03/using-data-to-drive-choices-in-math.html) also expanded upon the idea, deleting the names and numbers.

I think it is just great to use a Status of the Class chart as a student self-check-in that is not associated with the actual unit assessment. You

Figure 2.14 *I Can* Wall

I can/I am learning to			
	I am still learning to do this. I need lots of help still.	I can do this some. I still need a little bit of help.	I can do this well. I am an expert.
I can illustrate a fraction.	John, Tom, Raul, Maria, Sue, Larry, Carol, Sharon	David, Ricardo, Juan, Joe, Kiyana, Shakhira, Sue, Nancy, Marvin	Mike, Joshua, Grace, Jamal, Mary, Lucy, Brittany, Claudette
I can recognize equivalent fractions.			
I can generate equivalent fractions. 1/2, 2/4, 3/6			
I can compare fractions with the symbols <, >, and =. I can justify my comparisons with a visual model. 1/2 > 1/3			
I can order fractions. 1/5, 1/3, 1/2			

could put up a Math Data wall after the assessment that reflects what your students can and cannot do yet, but having a Status of the Class chart up throughout the unit of study will help your students to be cognizant and self-reflective about their own learning journey within the larger context. Your students can then identify and chart where they are in the process of learning this standard. Some teachers prefer to put up sticky notes with students' names, while others use dots with numbers (to keep it anonymous). Any of these scenarios works. Ideally, you should have discussions with your students about everyone being on their own journey so they do not feel any type of awkwardness from being in any of the categories. The big idea is that learning is a continuum, and everyone will move along the continuum the harder they try.

Math Bulletin Board

The math bulletin board is central to student learning. It is a display of what your students have done. Progressive bulletin boards are fantastic. A progressive bulletin board shows a student's various stages of understanding. For example, if a student gets a 1 or 2 on a scale of 4 (4 being the highest) the first time around, this number is put up on the board but at the bottom of the student's pile of work. As a student keeps trying, the student's efforts are displayed towards the top of his or her pile. So, there might be two, three, or more papers stapled together showing the student's progress towards mastery. This approach reflects the values of perseverance more than just putting a 2 up on the board with some comments.

Every student should get a chance at some point to pick what he or she wants to display up on the board to reflect his or her work in math class. Sometimes, teachers have a teacher's board and a students' board. The students are in charge of their board, and they display their choice of work. The teacher might have a different board with a particular theme or something.

Graffiti learning boards also work well. In this type of board, students put up thoughts, comments, and questions as they journey through a unit. They write on it much like one would write graffiti, and/or they could write on a post-it note. A graffiti learning board is more casual, but it documents the process of learning a particular topic. Students can write questions, put up comments, and reflect on "aha" moments. It is a space to collectively document their journey.

Key Points

- Create a math-rich environment:
  Meeting area
  Workstations
  Conference table
  Math schedule
  Calendar area
  Class clocks
  Math word walls
  Math data walls
  I Am Wall
  Bulletin boards
  Math manipulatives
  Student math thinking notebooks/class notebook
  Math library
  Folder center
- Anchor charts matter:
  Strategy charts
  Content charts
  Social charts

Summary

Classroom math environments set the tone for learning. They send messages about the importance of math. They provide tools that either promote or hinder student engagement all year long. Schedules should be clear. Routines should be explicit. Word walls, bulletin boards, and anchor charts all reinforce learning. The *I Can* and math data walls help students to focus on the current learning. The environment is part of the hidden curriculum; it teaches children something about the importance of math in the curriculum without ever saying a word. Make sure your room says, "Math is one of the most important things you'll ever learn."

Reflection Questions

1. What are some really strong elements of your math environment?
2. What are some parts of your math environment that you want to improve?
3. Is there a balance between your literacy anchor charts and your math anchor charts?
4. What new ideas stand out most for you in this chapter? What will you do next?

3

Managing the Workshop

Every moment invested in teaching routines is time well spent, because it will save hours of instructional time later.

Fountas and Pinnel, 1996, p. 62

Effective classroom management is the foundation to a successful Math Workshop. Children need to have a thorough understanding of the rituals and routines that make the classroom environment function smoothly. It is well worth the effort spent establishing rules, rituals, and routines the first few weeks of the school year so that you can actually have a fun-filled, academically rigorous, collaborative learning environment. Take the time to build the community so that the community can learn together. In terms of workstations, I tend to always use cooperative structures. Cooperative learning is the gateway into creating successful learning environments.

Cooperative Learning

Cooperative learning classrooms have specific elements woven throughout the lessons that ensure a great lesson. It is very distinguishable from group work, where children are just put in groups and teachers hope for the best. Johnson, Johnson, and Smith (1998) define cooperative learning as "the instructional use of small groups so that students work together to maximize their own and each other's learning." According to them, there are five elements that comprise a cooperative lesson (see Figure 3.1).

Classroom Management: Rules, Rituals, and Routines

Classroom management is about creating a community of learners who share a space and learn together. Children must learn from the very beginning to respect themselves, one another, and the teacher. They must also learn to help each other learn. In order to do these things, children

Figure 3.1 Five Elements of a Cooperative Lesson

Chart adapted from Johnson, Johnson, & Smith (1998)		
Positive Interdependence	Sink or Swim Together	"P" stands for Positive Interdependence, meaning that activities are designed in such a way that groups "sink or swim" together. This includes making sure that your students have individual roles, that they are working towards common goals, and that they share their resources. In terms of a numeracy workstation, this means that students are sharing materials, taking turns, and working together in their group in designated roles such as timekeeper, materials collector, cheerleader, and reporter. This becomes very important because when your students know who is going to do what, they are prepared for the situation. If they know that the class is working as a team and everyone knows what to do, then the class can be successful. This avoids arguments about who does what.
Individual Accountability	No Hitchhikers	"I" stands for Individual Accountability, meaning even if your students are doing group work, there are "no hitchhikers." Everybody is participating. Everybody knows what they are supposed to be doing and everybody is doing their fair share. In terms of a numeracy workstation, this means that your students are doing their own work. They are working in groups but they are accountable for the work and learning the skill sets they are practicing. They turn in individual artifact sheets of the work they did at the workstations, or they sign their name in the color they used to write the numbers on a group number chart.
Group Accountability	Teamwork	"G" stands for Group Accountability, meaning that the group takes responsibility for the way in which they worked together during workstation time. They sign a form that talks about the task work they did together as well as the teamwork. In kindergarten this could simply be circling happy faces or sad faces, whereas in second grade they might write a sentence about their task work and teamwork. This is one of the profound ways in which regular group work differs from cooperative work, because children are accountable for how they work together.

Figure 3.1 (Continued)

*Social Skills	Getting Along	"S" stands for Social Skills, meaning that the class is working on social skills as well as academic skills. This is another area in which group work differs from cooperative work. The idea is that social skills are taught as explicitly as academic skills. They are taught through a T-Chart. You will brainstorm this chart with the children so that when they are working together they understand what it means to share, work together, get along, and listen. In terms of a numeracy workstation, students are reminded that they are to be sharing and working together. Children don't just come to school with social skills. We have to teach them just like we teach reading, writing, and math skills, explicitly and with lots of practice. Role-plays help children learn and practice how to treat each other with actions and words.
Face-to-Face Interaction	Teamwork and Task Work	"F" stands for Face-to-Face interaction, meaning that the class is working on task work and teamwork. They are engaging in academically rigorous work that is improving their skill set, and they are making meaning together. They are scaffolds for each other. The idea is that together, students can learn much more than they ever could alone. In terms of a numeracy workstation, students are collaborating on activities, working together, and helping each other to practice the skills.
Sponge Activity	Meaningfully Soaking Up the Time	Sponge Activities are an important aspect of cooperative learning. This means that you have the next activity prepared in case students finish the workstation activities early. This prevents discipline problems from bored students, because they have something to do that is engaging and meaningful. In each workstation there is a folder for Finishers. It has quick activities your students can do if they finish. These might be dot to dots, number word searches, or add and color sheets.

*You brainstorm with the children what a specific skill looks like, sounds like, and feels like (see Figure 3.2). Post these ideas in a T-Chart and hang it in your classroom for ongoing reference. These charts should have words and pictures in the early childhood classroom.

Figure 3.2 Looking at the Skill of Sharing

Sharing		
What does it look like?	**What does it sound like?**	**What does it feel like?**
It looks like handing the glue to your partner.	Please	Happy
It looks like handing the crayons to someone.	Thank you	Fun
It looks like the things in the middle of you.	May I use	Nice

have to feel physically, emotionally, and socially safe. It takes time, energy, and effort.

Classroom management is also about building a sense of shared values, beliefs, rules, and routines that are explicit and consistent. It is important to have classroom rules and routines so that children know exactly what is expected of them when they are learning in their workstations. They need to know who is going to get the materials. They need to know who is going to report from their table for the day. They also need to have a designated person to get the teacher for help if needed.

Routines, Routines, Routines

Children need signals and procedures so learning can be engaging and spontaneous. They thrive in predictable environments. They need to know how to move their bodies and materials (McIntosh & Peck, 2005). Children work well when they know what to expect, when there are rules, rewards, and consequences, and when these are immediate and consistent from the beginning of the school year.

One of the biggest routines involved with Math Workshop is the transition times. Transitioning in and out of the different components of Math Workshop takes practice. One idea is to designate table leaders of the week who pick up the workstations and take them to their groups table, when this is appropriate. Other times, you can hand out workstations or have the children go to a specific spot in the room, such as the computer area. Workstation time usually lasts about 10–15 minutes for each rotation. This will always depend on your grade level and your class.

You should use different signals—sometimes visual signals, and other times verbal or musical ones. You must come up with a signal system that works well for you and your class. Thomas Armstrong (2009) talks about how it is important to use different signals that tap into a variety of intelligences. For instance, visual learners respond to signs written on the chalkboard or posters. Musical and linguistic learners respond well to singing and chanting routines. Bodily-kinesthetic learners enjoy clapping and hand movement signals. I have seen a xylophone used quite effectively. The sound is nice. The teacher hits it the first time to signal a 2-minute warning and to wrap up the work. When the students are ready, the table leader does the switching of stations. After one or two rotations, the children then transition to the rug for the debriefing/share time.

Hand Signals

Many teachers use hand signals as a communication system. It is efficient. Students raise a specified number of fingers based on their needs. For example, one finger might indicate that the student needs to go to the bathroom, two fingers might mean that the student has a question, and three fingers might mean that the student wants to get a tissue or water (see Figure 3.3). It is a good idea to have some basic ground rules around getting up. Encourage students to use the bathroom at recess. Discourage them from going to the bathroom during instructional time unless it is an emergency. Many teachers address this by having students go to the bathroom right after recess and right after lunch.

Figure 3.3 Our Classroom Hand Signals

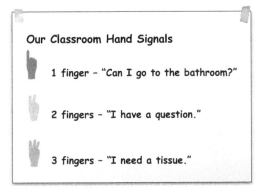

Clip art from Rebekah Brock (www.teacherspayteachers/Store/Rebekah-Brock). Used with permission.

Say What You Mean and Mean What You Say

I have found that it is important to be firm, consistent, and nice. Children should always know you care about them. When you scold Johnny for throwing the domino game piece across the room (especially if it is the fifth time), remember that he should feel that you like him but dislike what he is doing. Also, never threaten. For example, if you are working with a small guided math group and another group is acting up, don't threaten them by continuing to say, "If you guys don't get it together. . . ." If they don't have it together, give them an immediate consequence. Say what you mean and mean what you say. Don't give chances, because chances send the wrong message when it comes to classroom management. Children think "maybe there will be consequences if we are off task, and maybe there won't." If you have to take the table out of the station rotation for one round, then do it. Students tend to get the idea and correct the off-task behavior.

Finally, you can't take back what you give away. If you gave a table 5 points or 3 marbles, you can't take them back. What you can do is not give more. But if you start taking stuff back, you bankrupt your economy. Remember, with classroom management, consistency is the key.

Behavior

Classroom behavior should be established at the beginning of the school year. I believe that students should discuss what kind of community they want, write about it as a class, and then sign it. (Of course, you will guide the conversation so it has all the necessary items.) Remember that classroom rules should only and always be written in the positive. So write down what your students should be doing, not what they shouldn't be doing. Also, reinforce all the necessary behaviors with anchor charts about respect, getting along, and sharing.

It is important for you to address off-task behavior immediately. The rules and consequences should be explicitly clear. In Math Workshop, when your students are off task, their behavior should be explicitly addressed. Warnings are appropriate for some behaviors; however, when your students are doing dangerous behaviors like throwing things, remove them immediately from the station. For example, if a student is shooting rubber bands in the geoboard station, remove that student instantly. The student might not go back to that station for a while. The student has to reflect on his or her behavior, which includes filling out a form and then doing seatwork alone. Some teachers use checklists, others use forms that are more open (see Figure 3.4).

Figure 3.4 Student Behavior Reflection Tool

What I did . . .	Why I should not have done it . . .
What I will do next time . . .	Signatures: Student_____ Teacher_____ Guardians_____

Also, don't forget to emphasize the students that are doing good! You want to *catch them being good* (see Figure 3.5). There are many ways to celebrate this. One way is a circle map (discussed on http://teachinginroom6.blogspot). This is a big map with the names and acts of students caught in the act of being good. Some teachers make "Caught you being good" jars. Becca Foxwell has taken the "Bravo Board" a next step; she gives the team that earns the most points a Bravo Certificate that they can use to do special things.

Figure 3.5 Catch Them Being Good

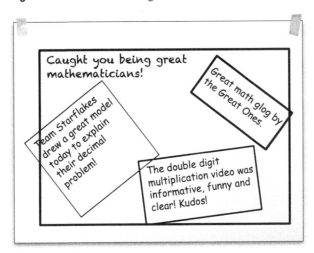

Tattling

Many people are using the Tattle Monsters, Tattle Turtles, and Tattle Bears to curb tattling in their classrooms (see Figures 3.6, 3.7, 3.8, and 3.9). The Tattle Monster is a creature created to receive tattles. Tattle Monsters are made out of trash cans, shoe boxes, and other materials. They are prominently displayed someplace in the classroom with a poem, a journal, and a pencil so students can write down their tattles.

Students are taught the difference between tattling and reporting, and whenever they have a tattle, they tell it to the monster (see Figure 3.6), the tiger, the turtle or the bear. One teacher even suggests that you hang a fake tail on the wall, and when the students come to you, tell them to go "tell the tail" (cited by A. Wolff, http://ashleywolff.org/2012/02/09/451/). Other teachers have a tattle telephone (where students dial 1 and log their complaint), and others have tattle books and jars. As with anything around classroom management, it is highly recommended that you role-play the difference between tattling and reporting with the students.

Figure 3.6 The Tattle Monster

The Tattle Monster

(Here to hear all your tattles!)

Tattle Monster

Says

"Tell me a tale

I'll listen long,

I'll listen good,

And I will listen well!

BUT, If your problem's really BIG

and DANGER you are in,

Tell a teacher immediately so they

can step right in!

Figure 3.7 Tattle to the Teddy

Tell the teddy. Then, put all
Tattles in the Box.

Figure 3.8 Books on Tattling

Here are some books to help you get started:

Tattlin' Madeline
Don't Squeal Unless It's a Big Deal: A Tale of Tattletales
A Bad Case of Tattle Tongue

Figure 3.9 Reporting vs. Tattling

Do you know the difference?		
Reporting	vs.	Tattling
Want to keep everyone safe	vs.	Trying to get someone in trouble
Need help from an adult	vs.	Can handle by yourself
Dangerous, disrespectful, hurts, mean	vs.	Not dangerous, nobody is getting hurt, it's not mean
Done on purpose	vs.	It was an accident
Important	vs.	Not Important/Just silly

The Great Pencil Challenge

Pencils are always a problem. They are one of the biggest "time sucks" in the classroom. I estimate that we spend about 40 hours talking about pencils throughout the year. Recently, several people have written posts and pins about "The Great Pencil Challenge." The basic idea is that you mark the pencils in some sort of way, and then at the end of the week, students are rewarded if they have their pencils. In a workshop in Austin recently, a teacher shared that she gives the students six pencils at the beginning of the week, and they are to return these pencils at the end of the week. So during the week, when one pencil gets broken, students just take another one from their pencil case. She said the students are really good about reminding each other that they don't need to go and sharpen pencils, because they have plenty.

Figure 3.10 The GREAT Pencil Challenge!

The GREAT
Pencil
Challenge!

Can you keep up with your 6 sharpened pencils all week long?
If you do you get a pencil award and you get your name entered into
the Great Pencil Raffle! Everybody's team that has all their original
pencils gets a team award! Are you up for the challenge?

Noise Levels

It is a good idea to have some sort of noise meter to monitor the noise levels in your classroom during Math Workshop. Math Workshop can be really loud. There are manual meters, paper meters, and virtual meters. Think about your class and get one so you can monitor the noise level. Have a student be the noise-level monitor who is in charge of moving the clothespin or marker up and down the chart (see Figure 3.11).

Figure 3.11 Chart on Noise Levels

5 Outside Talk
(use outside only)

4 Presenter Voice
(Tell us all
about it!)

3 Group Talk
(only your group
can hear you)

2 Partner Talk
(Whisper only
your partner
should hear you)

1 No Talking
(not a peep)

More Management Ideas

You can also use the "Use your words strategy," which is accompanied by props. When students are arguing, you say, "Use your words." Then you give them the language stems: "It bugs me when . . ." (student holds up a popsicle stick with a bug) and "I wish you would . . ." (student holds up a popsicle stick with a star) (see Figure 3.13). Another option is to just use cards. This comes from a great children's picture book about standing up for oneself called *A Bug and a Wish* (Scheuer, 2014).

Figure 3.12 Classroom Management Ideas

Classroom Management Ideas

Disagreements are inevitable. What is important is that you are prepared to handle them. You can set up certain structures in your classroom to help children have a place to solve disputes.

Idea	Materials	Strategy
Bambaloo Chair	Bambaloo Chair, Book, Pencil, Paper, Crayons	I recently saw a great strategy used by a first-grade teacher. There is a book called *Sometimes I'm Bambaloo*. It is the story of a little girl and how she acts when she is mad. She calls it "feeling Bambaloo" and describes her actions and their results in detail. So, the teacher read the book to her class and then set up a Bambaloo chair. She told the children that when they are feeling Bambaloo, they should go and sit in that chair. They have an opportunity to cool off and think about their feelings. I suggest you also put some pencils, crayons and paper near this chair so your students can draw out their emotions.
Peace Path	A path laid out in the classroom	This teacher also has a peace path set up in her room, where students are encouraged to walk with a friend and talk peacefully when they are having a disagreement.
Peace Table	A table with pencil, paper, crayons, and a stuffed animal	I have also seen a peace table, where the students go to talk out their problems with the help of a stuffed animal.
Class Meeting	A designated meeting time to discuss class business	Class meeting is a structure whereby classes meet together two or three times a week to discuss class business. Students can sign up on the agenda to address specific issues they are having with each other.

These are all structures to help navigate through the terrain of human relationships. They are all ways to get children to be in touch with their emotions and provide ways for children to express their emotions, without you having to come to the immediate rescue.

Figure 3.13 "Use Your Words" Strategy

Summary

Children thrive in safe, consistent, child-friendly, academically rigorous environments. They make meaning of math in classrooms where they are encouraged to actively construct their knowledge together. They work well when they know what to expect, how to behave, and genuinely feel like they are a valued member of the community. Always take the time to establish a community of learners so that your students may struggle and succeed together throughout the year.

Key Points

- Cooperative learning:
  Positive interdependence
  Individual accountability
  Group accountability
  Social skills
  Face-to-face interaction
- Rules and routines:
  Hand signals
  Variety of management signals
  Recognizing on-task behavior
  Consequences for off-task behavior
  Addressing tattling
  Addressing lost/broken pencils
  Addressing noise levels
- General management ideas:
  Bambaloo Chair
  Peace Path
  Peace Table
  Class Meeting
  A Bug and a Wish

Reflection Questions

1. Do you do much cooperative learning in your classroom? Do you often incorporate the five essential elements? How does this chapter push your thinking about these?
2. What social skills do your students need to work on?
3. How do you acknowledge on- and off-task behavior? What new ideas did you get from this chapter?
4. Which classroom management ideas can you see yourself immediately adopting, and why?

4

The Opening (Part I)

The Opening is the foundation of Math Workshop. Several important components of the overall workshop happen here such as: 1) calendar routines, 2) mathematical energizers, 3) fluency routines (like the number of the day or number talks), 4) problem of the day, and 5) the mini-lesson. Each of these components has a very particular purpose. You must be ever conscious of the mathematical takeaway for each component.

The Calendar

Calendar Math is really important but should take no more than 7–8 minutes. One of the most important aspects of Calendar Math is to get your students to realize that this is a routine about the everyday parts of their lives (see Figure 4.1). Your students will look at the weather, collect data about themselves and others, and count things that impact their day, like

Figure 4.1 Some Calendar Websites

Some calendar websites:

J Meacham has some wonderful ideas. See www.jmeacham.com/calendar/ calendar.htm. Be sure to look at the individual binder examples, because the author has posted the templates in both Word and PDF documents.

Scholastic has a great ideas page. See http://teacher.scholastic.com/fieldtrp/ k2/calendar.htm. One of the best ideas is to visit http://richardphillips.org. uk/number/ and to click on the number of the calendar day, and you will get tons of information about that number. Very cool!

Math Their Way has terrific calendar ideas. See www.center.edu/pub/docs/ Chapter4.pdf.

Mathwire. See www.mathwire.com./routines/morning.html. This morning routines page has great pictures: www.mathwire.com./routines/photos.html.

attendance and lunch. Your students should see the mathematical connections between how they live and what they learn about in school.

Calendar Math can help to reinforce those everyday skills that your students need to work on throughout the year. Your students will learn the days of the week, the months of the year, and the number of days in the school year. They will graph their teeth, their families, and different aspects of their lives. Your students will also work on their counting skills by ones, tens, hundreds, and so forth. Furthermore, they will talk about place value in different aspects, like making a number, writing a number, and grouping numbers for fast counting. Calendar Math should look different across the grades. After all, second graders know what day today is and what tomorrow will be! Frame your Math Calendar questions around the content of your grade level and the developmental appropriateness of your students.

Calendar Math can be done in a whole group. You can differentiate the instruction by having your students have individual calendar folders where they do varying levels of work. You can follow up with your students and look at these folders during individual conferences sometimes, just to do a check-in about their understandings. You could also pull small groups every so often to do some calendar binder work with them. In terms of differentiation, some children have two or three pages in their binder, whereas other students have four or five pages, depending on their readiness level.

One thing about Calendar Math is that it is really important to be clear and precise about the different types of graphs you are doing. If it is a pictograph, be sure to have a symbol. Oftentimes teachers graph the object, such as a dog, cat, or bird; but on most state exams, the pictograph has one symbol that the students use for all the votes (for example, a smiley face). Furthermore, on the bar graph, remember to label both axes, not just the categories and the numbers. The categories and the number names must be labeled, such as *Types of Pets* and *Number of Votes*. Also, be sure to put titles on your graphs. Then have your students make notes about the graphs by putting bubbles around the graphs. This is a great way to reinforce vocabulary.

Question of the Day

Question of the day is a great routine to do with students. It allows them to talk about data on an ongoing basis and pose and answer questions, see the shape of the data, and think about how people use data in real life. There are many ways to do question of the day. Some teachers have a station where they just change the question and the students use clothespins to vote (yes or no) on the question. Other teachers change the style of voting by the week, month, or chapter. For example, some weeks the students might vote by writing their name, other weeks by putting a sticky dot, and other weeks by putting up their picture. The questions and forms of collecting the data change depending on the grade level. In the upper elementary

Figure 4.2 Components of Primary Calendar (K–2)

Components of Primary Calendar (K–2)

SCHOOL CALENDAR/COMMERCIAL CALENDAR	COINS TO SHOW DATE	COUNTING JAR	TOOTH CHART OR BAR GRAPH	PLACE VALUE COUNTER
Have both calendars so your students can see the everyday calendar we use in real life. On the school calendar, reinforce patterns.	Use coins to display the date, because this will reinforce money concepts. I always have the students draw two ways to make the money in their journal.	It is important to have some sort of counting jar where your students can see the quantity grow. You can do this with a counting jar or a picture where students are putting some sort of sticker up every day.	It is good to have both a tally chart and a bar graph. One suggestion is to do a tally lost tooth chart and a weather bar graph. Keep them all up (perhaps stapled on top of each other) or presented in a line across the room so your students can compare the data across the year.	It is important to *emphasize* naming the number in a variety of ways. For example, 42 can be 4 tens and 2 ones, or 42 ones.
ODD AND EVEN COUNTERS	COUNT DOWNS	GROWING CALENDAR	DATE	BIRTHDAY GRAPH
You can use cubes and stack them by 2s to determine if the day is odd or even. This is a great visual tool.	These are fun to count down upcoming holidays. For example, you put up a turkey and 30 links, and the students remove a link each day to count down to Thanksgiving.	Whatever your system, students should be in charge of it. Some people use sticky notes and the students write the number and add it every day. Some people use a blank hundreds grid and the students add a number every day, while others use adding machine paper tape.	Some teachers have a frame that students fill out. Other teachers use some sort of markers (clothespin) and students clip the day of the week and use phrase stems like these: Today is _____. Yesterday was _____. Tomorrow will be _____. The month is _____. The year is _____. OR Today is _____. It is also written as ____/____/____. It is the _____ day of school.	Ideally this should be made into some sort of bar, tally, or pictograph so that students can see the shape of the data and ask math questions about it. Put the questions in bubbles with the student's name on it around the graph.

grades you might do this only once a week, whereas in kindergarten you might do it every day. The goal is to look at how people collect data and to show different forms of graphs and different ways to think about relevant questions based on the data. Also, some weeks students vote on things like "what is your favorite hot drink" (apple cider, hot chocolate, or tea), and then, based on the data, they have a "winter hot drink party." (See www.pinterest.com/drnicki7/question-of-the-day-this-is-a-great-routine-for-pr/ for many examples.)

Fluency Energizers and Routines

Fluency routines and energizers are foundational to Math Workshop. The NCTM states that:

> Computational fluency refers to having efficient and accurate methods for computing. Students exhibit computational fluency when they demonstrate flexibility in the computational methods they choose, understand and can explain these methods, and produce accurate answers efficiently. The computational methods that a student uses should be based on mathematical ideas that the student understands well, including the structure of the base-ten number system, properties of multiplication and division, and number relationships.
>
> (National Council of Teachers of Mathematics, 2000, p. 152)

Fluency routines and energizers, done over time, build fluency through talk, discussions, and games. The difference between a routine and an energizer is that a routine is a more formalized structure, like a number talk, whereas an energizer is more like a game. Some examples of these games include The Number Hokey Pokey (singing the Hokey Pokey using numbers) or Disappearing Dan (a game in which you draw a man called Dan; put math equations and numbers on his shirt, pants, pockets, hat, shoes; and, as your students talk about them, you erase them; thus, Dan eventually disappears).

Both routines and energizers:

- Build number sense
- Build vocabulary
- Build conceptual knowledge
- Build mathematical modeling skills
- Build procedural fluency
- Build strategic competence
- Build a strong mathematical disposition.

Fluency routines and energizers are both done for 5–10 minutes. They take a variety of forms and are played in many different ways—individual, partner, small group, or whole class.

A Closer Look at Fluency Energizers

Here are examples of some math fluency energizers:

Half It!—You give a group of students an even starter number. The kids verbally toss it around the room, with each child halving the number until the group gets to the first odd number. So, for example, you might say, "Starter number 1000." Trevor says 500, Mica says 250, Carlos says 125, and then you stop. You might say, "Starter number 2000." Michael says 1000, John says 500, . . . and they keep going till they can't go anymore. You might say, "Starter number 1/2." Carlos says 1/4, and then Trina says 1/8. A similar game is to play **Double It!** You give a starter number and the kids verbally toss it around the room, this time doubling the number.

Number Line It!—Draw an unlabeled number line and then have your students plot numbers. You tell your students to draw a number line within specific parameters. For example, you might say, "Start it with 500, end it with 1000 . . . write where 650 is . . . write where 899 is. . . ." You might say, "Draw a number line . . . start with 2/3 and end with 2 ½ . . . write where 1 ½ goes . . . write where 1 ¾ goes . . . write where 2 goes." Your students will really begin to learn number ranges with practice over time. Number lines are extremely important.

True or False—Put something on the board that is true or false and have the children debate it. For example, you draw a hexagon that doesn't look like the typical hexagon in the pattern block box, and the children have to debate whether or not that is a hexagon based on the properties of a hexagon. This activity is great because it gets children to think mathematically.

What Doesn't Belong—In this routine, you put a group of numbers on the board based on specific criteria, and then your students have to figure out what doesn't belong. In this routine, I ask the students to look at the numbers and to think to themselves for a minute. Then, I ask them to share their thinking with a partner, giving each person some time to explain his or her thinking. Next, I ask who wants to explain his or her thinking. Remember that this is a reasoning routine, so you should not just be interested in the answer, but more so in the students' reasoning behind the answer.

I Was Walking Down the Street—In this routine, you say, "I was walking down the street and I heard Tony say 15, and I wondered 'what was the question?' " The students then have to give an expression as an answer, such as, "Was it 5 × 3?" or "Was it 5 + 5 + 5?" or "Was it 15 – 0?" Then you begin to adjust the criteria, such as, "I was walking down the street and I heard Jamal say 12, and he didn't use any . . . addition, subtraction, multiplication" (the criteria will depend on the grade). This energizer

Figure 4.3 What Doesn't Belong

K–2 Example	Grades 3–5 Example
3 + 3 + 1 7 + 0 14 – 7 3 + 4 8 + 2 11 + 3	7 × 1/10 .07 .7 7/10 7
In looking at these numbers, students oftentimes will say things like, "3 + 3 + 1 doesn't belong" because it has 3 numbers. Or they will say 14 – 7 doesn't belong because it is a subtraction problem. I will respond that this is a great observation, but that is not my rule, so they must look again. Finally, they realize that the rule is 7, and so 8 + 2 doesn't belong.	This is difficult for many students wrestling with fractions and decimals. It is important to do reasoning activities where they have to talk out their thinking often.

is automatically differentiated because your students answer according to their math. They also hear others, and their thinking stretches. When their thinking stretches, they don't always reach. For example, I said the answer was 6, and one little first-grade boy said, "Was it 1000 – 994?" The students were very wowed by this, and so others tried. One little boy said, "Was it 20 – 15?" I never say no. I say, "Well, that will get us to 5, and we need to get to 6, so what are you going to do to get to 6?" Always throw the ball back to the student. Never do the reasoning for them. Make them think! When they think, they learn to stick with it, and their disposition grows!

A Closer Look at Fluency Routines

Number of the Day/Fraction of the Day/Decimal of the Day

What Is It?
Number of the day routines provide flexibility with numbers, fractions, and decimals. The basic idea is to take a number and then do different things with that number, like add it, subtract it, multiply it or divide it. Illustrate it with a model. Tell a story about it. There are so many different ways to do this. See Figure 4.4 for a few ideas.

Why Do It?
The number of the day is a quick routine that should take 2–3 minutes. Your students will do it in their journal and then share their answers with the class. Usually you will put up some type of anchor poster with the prompts on it for the class to think about. It develops computational fluency. It is crucial that even in kindergarten, students have their own number of the day template. Remember that whoever has the pen is the one learning. So if

Figure 4.4 Number of the Day Ideas

Number of the Day Ideas	
K–2	**Grades 3–5**
• Draw the number with base-ten block models • Double the number/half the number • Show the number with money • Show the number in a ten or double ten frame • Write the number in expanded form • Make the number using addition and/or subtraction • Add/subtract 10 or 100 to the number • Write the number name	• Draw the number with base-ten block models • Double the number/half the number • Find all the factors of the number • Find all the multiples of the number • Show the number with money • Write the number in expanded form • Make the number using addition, subtraction, multiplication and/or division • Show the number as an array • Draw a rectangle with a perimeter of this number • Draw a rectangle with an area of this number • Write the number name
Activities vary depending on the grade. Activities should be aligned to the standards. See many examples here: www.pinterest.com/drnicki7/number-of-the-day/	

Figure 4.5 Fraction of the Day and Decimal of the Day

Fraction of the Day (Grades 3–5)	Decimal of the Day (Grades 4–5)
• Decide if the fraction is in simplest form • Add 1/4 to the fraction; draw a model • Subtract 1/4 from the fraction; draw a model • Add 1/2 to the fraction (you want students to realize that this is easy . . . just decompose 1/2 into fourths); draw a model • Subtract 1/2 from the fraction (see above); draw a model • Multiply the fraction by 3/write a story to go with your equation • Compose/decompose the fraction . . . like 3/4 = 1/4 + 1/4 + 1/4 or 3/4 = 1/2 + 1/4 • Divide 3 by the fraction/write a story to go with your equation • Draw the fraction on a number line . . . is it closer to 0, 1/2, or 1? • Draw the fraction as a set and/or as the area model	• Write the decimal in word form • Write the decimal in fraction form • Write 2 decimals that are greater than this decimal (show them all on the number line) • Write 2 decimals that are less than this decimal (show them all on the number line) • Write the decimal in expanded form • Add .9 to this decimal • Subtract .9 from this decimal • Multiply 2 by this decimal/write a story about this equation • Round the decimal to the nearest tenth and hundredth • Compare the decimal with symbols to 2 other decimals
Activities vary depending on the grade. Activities should be aligned to the standards.	

Maria just watches and talks about the number of the day while the teacher or the student of the day does the writing, she will have a very different experience than if she does the writing every day.

Number Talks

What is it?

A number talk is a short 5- to 15-minute talk about numbers during which your students will talk about "number relationships and the structures of numbers to add, subtract, multiply and divide" (Richardson, 2011). Number talks are an integral part of the Math Workshop when you specifically work on the elements of fluency (speed and accuracy, flexibility, and efficiency). They are not necessarily correlated with the current unit of study, but they are in alignment with the fluency expectations of the given grade.

What Is the Goal?

The specific goal of a number talk is to develop "computational fluency." Your students will get the opportunity to discuss the many ways that they are looking at a problem and the many strategies that they are using to think about it. They also discuss in depth which of the strategies are efficient. Number talks will build your students' mental math capacities, because most of the work is done orally, although there are times when your students might record their thinking and talk from those notes. Also, many teachers, especially in the upper grades, want to start out by getting their students to record their thinking and then talk about it.

People do number talks in a variety of ways. You can talk about one expression, such as how to add $7 + 8$ or 26×17; or you can do a number string where you list a series of related problems, like 4×10, 4×100, and 4×1000. The important point is that you have to be very clear on the goal. It is important to think about how your students are reasoning about the problem, what models they are using to show their thinking, what language they are using to discuss their ideas, and whether they are seeing structure and patterns in the numbers. What is it that you want your students to walk away with from this session? Here is a format adapted from Math Perspectives (Richardson, 2011):

1. The teacher presents the problem
2. Students figure out the answer
3. Students share their answers (other students use different hand motions to agree or disagree with their thinking)
4. Students share their thinking (they discuss each other's thinking).

Math Perspectives makes some really important points about number talks that I think get lost in today's versions. The author notes that "the interaction between teacher and students should be like a conversation rather than a report . . . teachers help students clarify their thinking in several ways: by asking questions, by describing what the child did, and by writing down the process" (Richardson, 2011).

Let's look at a number talk:

Teacher: Today we are going to do a number talk about adding 1/2 and 5/8. Think about ways we might add these fractions together. When you have an idea, show me with your thumb up. Everyone remember to wait until everyone has had plenty of time to think. Ok, who would like to share their thinking?

Charles: I did 1/2 plus I know that 5/8 is really 1/2 + 1/8th. So I then added 1/2 + 1/2 = 1 whole and then had 1/8 left. (Several of the children motion a "me too" sign.)

Teacher: How many people solved it the same way as Charles? Ok. Who did it a different way?

Daniella: I made 1/2 into eighths. I know that 4/8 is a half, and adding that to 5/8 is 9/8, which is 1 whole and 1/8. (Many students motion a "me too" sign).

Teacher: Does everyone understand the two strategies we have just discussed? Who can come up and model one of those strategies with either an area model, like pattern blocks or the fraction circles, or with a linear model, like the number line or the fraction strips?

Taylor: I am going to do it with the fraction circles. (Taylor comes up and illustrates it with the magnetic fraction circles.)

Marta: I can model it with the fraction strips. (Marta comes up and illustrates it with the fraction strips.)

Teacher: Does anybody have another way to solve this?

Mateo: I can show it on the double number line. I am going to use 8 as the whole number part. I added them together and got 9/8. So it is 1 and an 1/8.

Figure 4.6 Double Number Line Example

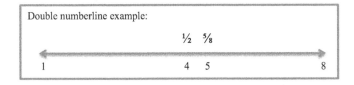

Teacher: Alright, so we have looked at three different ways to show this today. You all are doing some really powerful thinking. We are going to continue talking about fractions tomorrow.

You should do number talks at least two or three times a week, if not more. In the primary grades, be sure to "subitize" every day. "Subitizing" is showing your students quick images of numbers, usually 1–10. This is the foundation for adding and subtracting. This routine should be done with ten frames, scattered dots, in a line, in a circle, and in domino formations. There are many free resources, both virtual and paper, to start or expand this routine (see www.pinterest.com/drnicki7/subitizing/). Students should talk about what they see instead of just saying how many dots there are. The emphasis is on students composing and decomposing numbers. They should be able to talk about how 6 can be 3 and 3, or 5 and 1, or 6 and 0.

Shape of the Week

Another type of number talk is a geometry talk. In this talk, you will show quick images of shapes. When your students see the shapes, they have to describe them, such as, "I saw a shape with six corners and six sides." The students are not allowed to name the shape until they have named three or four different attributes of the shape. This builds an understanding of attributes and should be done at least once a week throughout the year. Teachers tend not to stress geometry except in the geometry unit, so students often don't have a deep understanding of shapes.

A Different Type of Number Talk

There is a different type of number talk that I recently saw on a video by The National Centre for Excellence in the Teaching of Mathematics. In this video, second-grade students are talking about subtraction. The framework for the discussion is quite interesting. On the board is a template that looks like this:

Figure 4.7 Template for Number Talk

I can do it in my head.	I can do it with a model.	I need to figure it out with a written method.
		3/5 – 1/10
		3/5 = 6/10
		6/10 – 1/10 = 5/10

1/2 3/6
5/8 2/5
9/7

1/4 1/3
1/8 4/7
2/14
1/10

Adapted from the National Center for Excellence in the Teaching of Mathematics (2014).
https://www.ncetm.org.uk/resources/40532

In this vignette, the students discuss the subtraction of these fractions:

Teacher: Everyone look at the fractions that we have on the board today. I want you to think about these fractions. Remember that you will pick a fraction from the first circle and then a fraction from the second circle to subtract. Then, tell us how you solved the problem. Did you do it in your head? Did you have to make a model? Did you use a written method?

Tiffany: I subtracted 1/4 from 1/2 in my head. That was easy because I know that 1/2 is 2/4 so I just took away 1/4 and I had 1/4 left.

Teacher: So how did you know that 1/2 is equivalent to 2/4?

Tiffany: Because I know my equivalent fractions. That is an easy one.

Luke: I did 3/6 minus 1/3. I did it in my head. I made 1/3 into 2/6 by multiplying it in my head and I found the difference between the two fractions. It is 1/6.

Teacher: Why did you multiply it?

Luke: I needed to get like denominators so I could subtract.

Maria: I did 5/8 – 1/4 but I did it with calculations. I multiplied 1/4 by 2 to get eighths and then I subtracted 2/8 from 5/8. I got 3/8.

Teacher: So, your strategy was the same as Luke's, only you did it with the actual calculations on the paper. Mmmmm . . . These are all great ways to think about these numbers. I like the way you can name exactly what you did.

Tom: I drew a double number line to solve 2/5 – 1/10. I know that 2/5 equals 4/10. So I just hopped back 1/10 and got 3/10.

Figure 4.8 Number Line Example

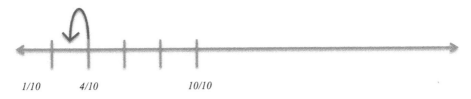

1/10   4/10   10/10

Teacher: So Tom, if I hear you correctly, you thought about it as a subtraction problem and used the number line to support your thinking.

Tom: Yes.

This is an excellent talk structure because it allows the children to reflect on and name the strategy they are using to solve problems. We normalize this type of talk by having specific structures in place for students to practice this. As a follow up, you can pull small guided math groups and work with your students on these same problems in order to hear everybody's thinking. This is also a great structure to put in a workstation.

Problem of the Day

The problem of the day is a time for your students to engage deeply with rich tasks. The problem of the day is no longer a 10-minute quickie. You should provide a rich problem that might take a few days to explore. On the first day, your students might discuss the problem. On the second day, your students might talk about laying out a pathway, models they might use, tools they might need and what the general plan could be. On the third day, your students might try to solve the problem one way and check their answer another way. On the fourth day, your students might write about how they did it. And on the fifth day, everyone might share their journey. Of course, all problems of the day aren't going to take this long, but you need to really spend time getting your students to "plan a solution pathway rather than just jumping to a solution" (CCSS, 2010).

Figure 4.9 Decontextualizing

> Decontextualizing
>
> Sara has 5 rings. Kate has 2 more rings than she does. How many rings do they have altogether?

Figure 4.10 Contextualizing

> Contextualizing
>
> 5 rings is the answer. What was the question? (It was a division problem).

The problem of the day should also be about reasoning out the problem. This would mean that sometimes you give your students a word problem and they then have to figure out an equation to solve the problem (in other words, decontextualize: go from words to numbers). Other times, you should give your students an equation and ask them to come up with the problem (in other words, contextualize: go from numbers to words). You should give your students an opportunity to contextualize problems at least once a week. Here is a snippet of a contextualizing conversation:

Teacher: Hello class. Today, 5/8 is the answer. What is the question? Everybody think about that for a minute and jot some ideas in your Thinking Notebook. After a few minutes, ask your students to turn to their designated math partner and take turns sharing their answers. After this, ask the children to share their thinking with the class.

Jennifer: I put that Sue ate 2/8 of a pizza for breakfast and 3/8 for lunch. How much pizza did she eat all day?

Teacher: What do you all think of that problem?

Joe: I did a pizza problem too. That is a good problem.

Timothy: I did a pizza problem but it was a little different. I put that Joe ate 1/2 a pizza at lunch and then 1/8 for dinner. How much did he eat all total?

Teacher: Let's talk about these two fraction problems. Can they both be correct?

Claire: Yes, because you can break apart a fraction in a lot of ways. Like the other day when we were doing our number talk.

Tom: Yes, I thought about the number talk too. Ok, so I started with a pizza that had 8 slices. I put that there were 5 kids at the birthday party and they each had one piece of pizza. How much pizza did they eat?

Sharon: Or you could make it a subtraction problem. Like, there was a pizza with 8 pieces and the kids ate 3. How much was left?

Teacher: This is excellent thinking. I want you all to be sure to draw a model for your problems. Remember that there are three types of basic models . . . you could use an area model like the pattern blocks, fraction squares, or fraction circles. Or, you could use a set model with the counters or tiles. Or, you could use a linear model with the number line or the fraction strips. Remember that it is really important to be able to draw a model to illustrate your thinking. I am now going to give you 3 minutes to jot down a model and explain how you solved your problem. Also, remember—I can't see inside your brain. You have to write clearly, what you did exactly, why and how. Also, be sure to use your math words!

Remember that the problem of the day is a routine that is about getting students to understand the process of problem solving, and that discussions should be about way more than the procedure. Your students should understand the importance of solving one way and checking another, as well as "double double checking" their answer.

Summary

The Opening is the first part of Math Workshop. It takes up about 20 to 30 percent of the workshop, and it is extremely important. You do the Calendar Math, daily fluency routines and energizers, the problem of the day, and the mini-lesson (which we will discuss in detail in Chapter 5). During this part of the day, the children are warming up, practicing the essentials and getting on friendly terms with numbers. Children are learning to think fast, flexibly, and efficiently. They are learning to express their mathematical ideas as well as listen to the mathematical ideas of others. They are becoming better mathematicians. Going from good to great happens a lot in the daily routines of the opening. Be sure to utilize this time well, giving your students the skills they will need to become confident and competent mathematicians.

Key Points

- Calendar math
- Question of the day
- Fluency energizers and routines:
  Half It!
  Double It!
  Number Line It!
  True or False?
  What Doesn't Belong?
  I Was Walking Down the Street
  Number of the Day
  Fraction of the Day
  Decimal of the Day
  Shape of the Week
  A Different Type of Number Talk

Reflection Questions

1. What daily energizers and routines do you currently do to build computational fluency with your students? What new ideas do you have after reading this chapter?
2. In thinking about the way that you teach fluency, do you work on all three elements—speed and accuracy, flexibility, and efficiency? Do you emphasize one over the other, or do you strike a pretty good balance? What new ideas do you have about teaching the three elements?
3. What do you currently do with problem of the day? Are you doing microwave problems that students can solve in 2 minutes, or are you giving rich tasks that require planning out a solution pathway?

5

The Opening (Part II)
Mini-Lessons

Mini-lessons are portals into powerful thinking.

Newton, 2014

Whole-group mini-lessons lay the foundation for the Math Workshop. They invite your students to think about real-life math in meaningful ways. They should excite, thrill, intrigue, and invite your students to wonder. It is here that you will introduce big ideas, procedures, reasoning, strategy, and general discussions about the ways of being and acting like mathematicians. These lessons should captivate your students, make them sit on the edge of their seat and wonder, "What will we learn today?"

What Are the Goals of Mini-Lessons?

Whole-group mini-lessons have different goals. You should frame the mini-lessons around the goals of mathematical proficiency. You can design them to build conceptual understanding, procedural fluency, strategic competence, adaptive reasoning, and mathematical disposition.

What Is the Teacher's Role in a Mini-Lesson?

Your role as the teacher is to facilitate the learning around the desired goal. You will frame the mini-lesson for your class. You will talk about what the class is going to talk about. You will set clear expectations around the mathematical takeaways of the lesson. You will also work as a coach during the discussions, prompting your students appropriately.

What Are the Students' Roles During a Mini-Lesson?

Students are involved in different ways. They could be doing math in written form, mentally, verbally or acting it out. Students are definitely an active part of the mini-lesson. They have to be taught the expectations for their behavior in the mini-lesson. Mini-lessons are active, engaged, hands-on, minds-on spaces where students are thinking out loud and publicly participating in a math encounter.

What Do Whole-Class Mini-Lessons Look Like?

Whole-class mini-lessons are framed around the five components of mathematical proficiency. They can take on a variety of formats, including picture books, videos, songs/chants, poems, discussions, interactive lectures, and a variety of 21st-century technologies.

Structural Framework: Working on the Big Ideas

There are a variety of types of mini-lessons. These are scaffolded around the five components of mathematical proficiency. So, whatever your format, you are trying to build competence in one of these five areas: conceptual, procedural, strategic competence, adaptive reasoning and/or mathematical dispositions.

Conceptual Mini-Lessons

In these types of mini-lessons, you are teaching children about a concept. You are working on the big ideas and the enduring understandings. For example, in the primary grades, you might do a concept lesson on understanding that people talk about shapes by discussing their attributes. In a conceptual mini-lesson, you might use the format of visual prompting. A really good book series for teaching shapes is the Tana Hoban series. So, you might use the book *Circles and Squares* and do a picture walk through that book. It is a great book because it has great visual pictures. Conceptually in this lesson, you are trying to get your students to understand that circles and squares can look a lot of different ways, but they have some distinguishing features. Let's listen in on a conversation:

> **Teacher:** Hello everybody. I have a book here that is so fantastic that I want to share with you. Let's take a picture walk. I want you all to look at it closely and tell me what you notice.

An example of a conceptual lesson in third grade might use videos as a format. You could show at least two or three videos over a few days, and then have your students fill out a protocol and engage in discussion about what a fraction is based on what they have seen. You want your students to use digital information to inform their thinking about this concept. Through the digital information and the scaffolded conversations, your students will begin to define what a fraction is and what a fraction is not.

Procedural Mini-Lessons

Procedural mini-lessons teach students how to do the math. The lessons might be about a particular algorithm or strategy. They could also be about how to draw or illustrate a concept. For example, in second grade, you might do a lesson on how to draw a number line to model thinking. This would include introducing the open number line, talking about how the class might use it, and then modeling how to use it. This mini-lesson would be part of a series of mini-lessons on the open number line and might take three or four lessons to teach.

Figure 5.1 An Open Number Line

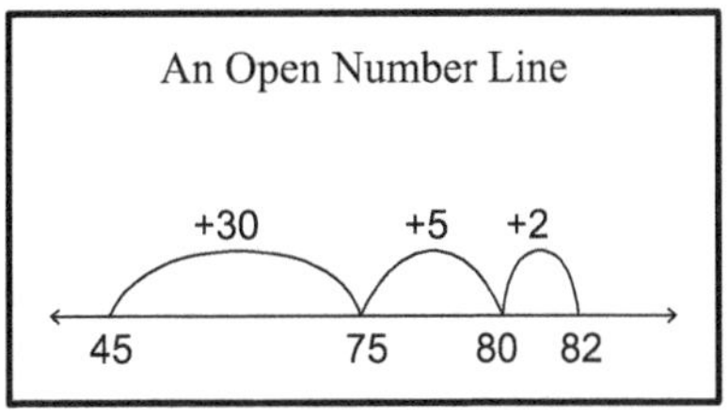

An Open Number Line

+30   +5   +2

45   75   80 82

An example of a fourth-grade procedural fluency lesson would be introducing the open array for division. This lesson involves teaching students how to set up the array and then how to go about the procedure of finding friendly numbers/compatible numbers to solve the array. This mini-lesson would be part of a series of mini-lessons on the open array for division, and scaffolded over a few days with different numbers.

Strategic Competence

Strategic competence lessons teach students how to use various strategies. There is a huge emphasis on using strategic competence and using flexible strategies in many state standards. There are even levels of strategies for addition, subtraction, multiplication, and division. Many state standards require that students not only can use the general method (traditional method), but also specialized strategies based in place value and properties. There is an emphasis on students having a variety of strategies to do the operations.

Figure 5.2 Addition Strategies

Addition Strategies

Adding 0
Adding 1
Counting on 1, 2, 3
Make Ten
Doubles
Doubles + 1
Doubles + 2
Adding 7, 8 or 9

For example, in a second-grade classroom, you might do a lesson on different ways to add 37 + 8. In this lesson, you would present the problem and ask your students what kinds of models they might use and what strategies they might use. Here is a snippet:

Teacher: Here is an expression. Now, you guys know a lot about adding single-digit numbers. When you look at this problem, what do you see and what do you know?
Student: I see 7 + 8. I know that 7 + 8 is 15.
Teacher: Excellent! What else do you see in this problem?
Student: I see that there are 3 tens and I know that 15 + 30 is 45.
Teacher: Ok. So, one way to find this answer is to add the ones and then the tens. Can anybody think of another way to do it?
Student: You could make the 8 a 10 and the 37 a 35.
Teacher: Tell me more about how you did that?
Student: I saw a lucky 8 so I made it a 10. To make it a 10 I had to take 2 from 37 to make it 35. So that makes . . . 35 and 10 . . . 45.
Teacher: Who agrees with her?

Continue the conversation about ways to add 37 + 8. This type of thinking takes public practice. Your students hear it and see it because the thinking is made visible by the public record that you are recording as the students are speaking.

An example of an upper elementary grade is doing a lesson on multiplication fact strategies. For example, in many third-grade math algebraic operations and thinking standards, there is an emphasis on students being able to multiply using the different properties. Students don't just know how to do this; they have to see it taught, talked about, and practiced. So in this lesson, you would give an interactive lecture on multiplying with strategies:

Teacher: Hi everybody. Today we are going to talk about our number 8 timetables. We have been studying our 2s and 4s. Who wants to summarize the conversations we have been having about that? [you record student thinking on board here]
Student A: Well, we were talking about how 2s and 4s are related. Like, if you don't know your 4s you can think 2s (like it says on the poster up there).
Student B: Yeah, like, say I don't know 4 × 5. I could think 2 × 5 and double it. I would get 20.
Teacher: Ok, so does anybody have another example?
Student C: Yeah, like 2 × 8 is 16, so 4 × 8 is 32. It's just double. You just double everything for the 2s to get the 4s.
Teacher: Ok, now I am thinking about my 8s today. Who can tell me about how 8 is related to 4?

Student D: It's double. 8 is double 4.

Teacher: So, do you think we could do the same type of strategy we were doing for 4s with the 8s?

Student E: Of course.

Teacher: Ok, who wants to try thinking about it out loud?

Student C: I do. . . . If 4 × 1 is 4 . . . then 8 × 1 is 8 . . . it's double . . . or if 4 × 2 is 8, then 8 × 2 is 16 . . .

Student F: I got one, 4 × 5 is 20, so 8 × 5 is

Student G: 40.

Teacher: You guys got it . . . let's look at some of what we have said . . .

A strategic competence mini-lesson is about getting your students to talk about their math strategies. It is important to spend time every week during Math Workshop just talking and listening to each other's thinking. Thinking out loud and listening to each other carefully is the glue that holds the workshop together. Your students have to see a variety of strategies and listen to a variety of strategies to begin to develop a toolkit of strategies that they are comfortable with. The idea is not that every child learns every strategy. The idea is that every child is exposed to a variety of strategies, that they learn there is more than one way to do something, and that some ways are more efficient than others.

Reasoning

Adaptive reasoning is about getting your students to think. Mini-lessons that get students to think deeply about something, reason it out loud, and listen to others are really important to do. Of course, teachers do this all the time, but I am talking about some specific routines that build reasoning intentionally. For example, reading and making sense of two arguments. Let's listen to this second-grade conversation:

> **Teacher:** Good morning. Today is Two-Argument Tuesday. I am going to show you two arguments and you brilliant mathematicians are going to figure out what is happening. First, I want you to read each argument carefully. Then I want you to think about what you read. Then you will have an opportunity to discuss it with a partner. Then we'll talk about it. Be ready to defend your thinking. Here goes:

Figure 5.3 Sample Argument

Susie and Carla went to the store. They both bought lollipops for $.25. They both gave the cashier $1. Susie got back two quarters and two dimes and a nickel. Carla got back 3 quarters. Susie said she got back more money because she got more coins. Carla said they got the same amount just in different coins. Who is correct and why?

Teacher: Ok, share your thinking with your partner. Be sure you can defend it. Who wants to restate the situation?

Gabby: There are two girls. They went to the store and bought some candy. They gave 25 cents and a dollar. I mean they gave a dollar to pay . . . the candy was 25 cents. They got change back.

Teacher: Ok, so what is the question we are thinking about?

Gabby: Who got more money . . .? I think Susie.

Dan: I think Susie is right because she got more money.

Nina: No, but it is the same because three quarters is 75 cents and Susie has two quarters, which is 50 cents, and then one dime is 60 and then another is 70 and a nickel is 75.

Jose: I agree with Nina … they both make 75 cents.

Teacher: Ok, is there a model we could use to prove it?

Nina: I'll prove it on the number grid.

Carlos: I will prove it on the open number line.

Conversations like the one above help students to reason out loud, listen to the arguments of others, choose sides, follow logic, and defend their thinking. This happens with time and practice. It is part of an overall culture of becoming great mathematical thinkers.

Mathematical Disposition

In a mathematical disposition mini-lesson, students talk about their learning trajectory. They talk about themselves as learners and what it takes to be a good mathematician. These are lessons that talk about the habits of mind and the ways of being that great mathematicians exhibit. They ask students to reflect on their current learning and to plan for their future learning. Let's listen into a kindergarten conversation:

Teacher: (Around April) Good afternoon everybody. Today we are going to talk about thinking about our thinking. I want you to listen to me think about my thinking and plan my next steps. I am thinking about the strategies that I use when I model my thinking. When the paper says show my thinking, I use the ten frame a lot. That is one of my go-to models. I think I am going to try to use the number line more. Ok, I want you all to think about which model you use all the time. Maybe you can think of another model that you would like to try. Let's look at our model poster. Look at all of these models. Look at them and think about which one you use all the time. Talk about that with your math partner. Ok, who wants to share with the group?

Mario: I use the number line.

Tammy: I use the ten frame.

Tiffany: I use the rekenrek.

Teacher: Now, look at the poster again . . . think of another model that you want to start using more . . . talk about that with your math partner.

Elise: I am going to try to use the ten frame.

Eddie: I am going to try to use the number line.

Terri: I am going to try to use the number line too.

The purpose of mathematical disposition mini-lessons is to get your students to reflect on themselves as mathematicians. We need to take more time to allow our students to think about their thinking and their habits as mathematicians. We need to engage in structured conversations that get students talking about what they are doing and how they are doing it. We can give our students lots of things, but one of the most important things we can give them is the confidence to do math well throughout their lives.

Whole-Class Mini-Lesson Formats That Work

Picture Books

Picture books can be a great springboard into talking about the big ideas in math. There are several great picture books, as well as picture book series, that teach mathematical concepts. We live in a "storied" society—meaning that we love stories, we tell stories, we listen to stories, and most importantly, we frame our lives around stories. Math stories help the math make sense to students.

For example, a great math picture book to use in primary grades is *Quack and Count*. In this book, a mother duckling is counting her seven ducklings. The ducklings are lined up in different configurations. Mother duck counts six and one, five and two, four and three, and so forth. This is a great book to talk about ways to make numbers. This might be an extended mini-lesson, meaning that you would revisit it over a couple of days. On the first day, you might read the book and the class would have a discussion about what is happening in the story. On the second day, you might review the big idea of showing a number in different ways and then have your students act out the story. On the third day, you might review the big idea and have your students act out the story with manipulatives at their desk. On the fourth day, the children might change the number and draw on their white boards some stories to match this new number. These would all launch activities that could be continued in both guided math groups and Math Workstations.

An example of a great picture book for use in upper elementary grades is *Amanda Bean's Amazing Dream* (Neuschwander, 1998). This is a hilarious story about a little girl who loves to count but refuses to learn how to multiply. Through a series of silly events that happen in her dreams, she realizes the need to learn to multiply. This book is an excellent launch into the concept of multiplication. It looks at equal groups and arrays. It provides plenty of opportunity to practice some of the scenarios in the book and write number stories based on those scenarios. This book might only be read as a mini-lesson one day, and then the follow-up activities taken directly to guided math groups and Math Workstations.

The point here is that there are a variety of math picture books that offer plenty of mathematical information that "sticks" with children. You should definitely take full advantage of using this engaging instructional strategy to launch mini-lessons. One of the important things to remember about using math literature is to pull out the math! This is not just a language arts lesson, although the books could be used in both blocks. But in math class, you are not just looking at character, setting, and plot. You are looking at, discussing and trying to understand the math. You should make planning time to find the math, pull out the big ideas, scaffold the key questions, and outline the major takeaways from the experience.

Figure 5.4 Three Websites with Great Math Book Bibliographies

---

Three Websites with Great Math Book Bibliographies

www.mathsolutions.com/documents/lessons_chart-2.pdf
www.k-5mathteachingresources.com/ (they have books to go with different standards)
www.pinterest.com/drnicki7/books-worth-reading/ (not just this board but throughout the topic boards there are books pinned on each one about the topic).

Figure 5.5 Four of My Favorite Math Picture Books

Four of My Favorite Math Picture Books

Primary:
A Number of Dinosaurs by Paul Stickland.
A Quarter from the Tooth Fairy by Holtzman and Day.

Upper Elementary:
The Best of Times by Greg Tang.
Cut Down to Size at High Noon by Sundby and Geehan.

"Combining math and literature in classroom activities is a way for teachers to invite children into the world of math," stated Marilyn Burns (as cited in Bafile, 2001).

> Reading books that weave mathematical ideas into engaging stories helps dispel the myth that math is dry, unimaginative, and inaccessible. Children's books can not only generate interest in math but also provide contexts that help bring meaning to abstract concepts. Using children's literature is a win-win—for children and for teachers.
>
> (Bafile, 2001)

Videos

Videos are another way to launch mini-lessons. Students should get mathematical information from a variety of resources, including digital ones. One way to do this is to use videos to introduce big ideas. In the primary grades, this could look like using many of the Sesame Street videos to discuss early number concepts. These videos are all online and free now. Some of the best ones are the early ones from years ago. Also, a variety of other number sense, measurement and geometry informational videos can be pulled from various sites on the Internet including YouTube, SchoolTube and TeacherTube.

In the upper elementary grades, students watch a series of videos about a specific topic— for example, how to multiply fractions. Each day for the mini-lesson, they can talk about the big idea and then watch it presented in different ways. Show three videos about the topic and then have your students discuss their understanding each day in-depth with a partner and in a whole-group discussion. All of your students should have a viewing protocol so they can take notes. Explain to your students that a protocol is a way of keeping track of the information they are getting from the various videos. Figure 5.6 gives an example of a video viewing protocol.

Figure 5.6 Video Viewing Protocol

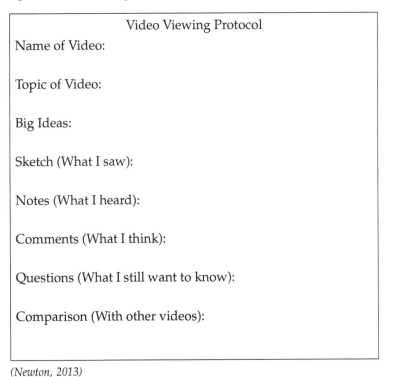

Video Viewing Protocol

Name of Video:

Topic of Video:

Big Ideas:

Sketch (What I saw):

Notes (What I heard):

Comments (What I think):

Questions (What I still want to know):

Comparison (With other videos):

(Newton, 2013)

Before your students watch the video, give them a quick oral review of the protocol. Then, they watch the video. In the beginning, you should pause the video along the way to give your students time to fill out the protocol. As time goes on, students are normalized into filling out the protocol as they are watching the video. After the video, give your students more time to fill out the protocol and discuss it with their math partner. Afterwards, everyone will come together and discuss their protocols. The emphasis is on the big ideas in the video, how these ideas are presented and how they build knowledge about the concept.

Figure 5.7 Three Sites for Teaching Videos

> **Three Sites for Teaching Videos**
>
> Learn Zillion: https://learnzillion.com/
>
> Math Playground: www.mathplayground.com/
>
> Khan Academy: www.khanacademy.org/

Songs/Chants

Songs and chants are great ways to introduce and reinforce concepts. Songs and chants provide mnemonic tools for students to learn concepts and practice them. Songs and chants give students an opportunity to act out physically—with manipulatives, with pictures and with numbers—their understanding of different mathematical concepts.

Figure 5.8 Three Places to Get Songs and Chants

> **Three places to get Songs and Chants**
>
> www.songsforteaching.com
>
> www.sparklebox.co.uk/maths/#.VXNdqmRViko
>
> www.canteach.ca/elementary/songspoems.html

In the early grades, students can sing songs like "Five Little Ducks," "Five Green and Speckled Frogs" and "Five Little Monkeys." Students sing the songs and then act out the concepts. While some students are acting out a song, the rest of the class is singing. In the upper elementary grades, students can sing songs and say chants that help them to remember concepts. For example, to teach students the strategy of compensation, meaning they adjust numbers to make them more friendly to add, I teach the students the two songs "Lucky 8" and "Lucky 9" (Newton, 2013).

Figure 5.9 Lucky 8

> **Lucky 8**
>
> You're so Great
>
> When I see you
>
> I know what to do
>
> I go to the other number
>
> And I take 2!

Figure 5.10 Lucky 9

Lucky 9
You are so fine
When I see you
I am almost done
I go to the other number
And I take 1!

These are simple poems that teach a concept. The students chant these poems and then practice the strategy. You can put up number strings (Fosnot & Uttenbogaard, 2008) (these are intentionally chosen problems) and have your students practice the concept.

Figure 5.11 Number Strings

8 + 6 = ?	18 + 7 = ?	48 + 19 = ?	138 + 27 = ?	148 + 26 = ?

Another example of a strategy chant is Neighbor Numbers.

Figure 5.12 Neighbor Numbers Strategies

Neighbor Numbers sit beside one another
Neighbor Numbers are as close as sisters and brothers!
They're all together tricky
Use them to add math quickly
Neighbor Numbers sit beside one another

Let's look at an example
On the number line
When you see them sittin' there
You know it's gonna be fine

Neighbor Numbers sit beside one another
Neighbor Numbers are as close as sisters and brothers!
They help us to add quickly
There really is no trickery!
Neighbor Numbers sit beside one another
Neighbor Numbers are as close as sisters and brothers!

←——————————————→
1 2 3 4 5 6 7 8 9 10

So let's add 3 and 4.

We know that 4 is 3 + 1 so:
  3 + 4
  3 + 3 + 1

It is a neighbor number! Use your double fact!

Interactive Lecture

In this type of a mini-lesson, you directly teach your students something that you want them to know. It isn't a "sit and get." Your students will be intellectually engaged active participants. They will be very much involved throughout the mini-lesson. The mini-lesson is built around the Hunter 7-step lesson plan. In this lesson plan, there is a hook and then an introduction of the topic, which is followed by a direct modeling of a particular idea, and then guided practice and checking for understanding. Then students do more guided practice in math centers and guided math groups. Eventually, the concepts in the mini-lesson are given to students for independent practice.

Hattie (2009) has shown that direct instruction has a statistically significant effect size of .82 on student achievement. What this means is that direct instruction has its place as one of many effective strategies in the math classroom. Direct Instruction with an interactive twist helps the lesson stick. SERC notes that "engagement triggers and tasks for interactive segments" are what keep the flow of the teaching going (http://serc.carleton.edu/sp/library/interactive/triggers.html). There are a variety of strategies that can be used as engagement triggers, such as think-pair-share, think-draw-share, turn and talk and the 1-minute essay (where students write for 1 minute everything they know about a topic). Let's listen in on an interactive lecture mini-lesson:

> **Teacher:** Hello everybody. Today we are going to be looking at these tools. They are called Fraction Strips. They are another way to model fractions. We had been looking at fraction circles and squares. Now, we are going to look at Fraction Strips. Tell me what you notice about them.
>
> **Student A:** They are all the same size but cut into different pieces like the circles.
>
> **Teacher:** Yes . . . they are . . . does anybody want to add to that noticing?
>
> **Student B:** There are halves and thirds and fourths and eighths.
>
> **Student C:** And tenths.
>
> **Teacher:** Wow, I am impressed at the fraction language that you all are using. So, this is called a linear model. . . . it is the same type of model as the number line. We have done some work with the number line. So this is another type of model and we are going to be doing various explorations with this model. What are some things you can do with this model? Think about what we did with the fraction circles and squares.
>
> **Student D:** You can compare the fractions . . . like 1/2 is the same as 2/4. . . .
>
> **Teacher:** Yes, we can compare . . . who could give me another example?
>
> **Student E:** 5/10 is equivalent to 1/2.
>
> **Teacher:** Yes, you are correct. So we can compare and we can do that by thinking about the size of the fraction and then even laying the

strips right beside each other. We will be doing some of all of these things. But first, we are going to make our own.

So, in this interactive lecture, the teacher has some specific information that she wants the students to know. She is introducing a new model for fractions. However, the mini-lecture is very interactive, and students are involved throughout.

Visual Prompts

Visual prompts are visual scaffolds, like photographs and physical props. You can use these to frame mini-lessons. You would put up these discussion starters and then facilitate a discussion around the prompt. For example, if you are talking about shapes, you could put up pictures of shapes in real life and then ask your students to talk about them based on shapes' attributes. These can be great mini-lesson launchers; students are so engaged because the lesson is immediately connected to real life. These are the components of the protocol:

1. Show the Visual Prompt
   - Introduce it

2. Discuss the Prompt: Open Conversation
   - Describe it
   - Think about what it tells us about math
   - Think about what it has to do with math

3. Final Thoughts
   - Comments
   - Questions
   - Things to think about

Figure 5.13 shows some examples of visual prompts.

Figure 5.13 Sample Visual Prompts

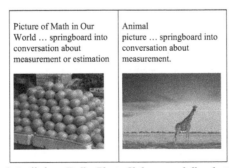

| Picture of Math in Our World ... springboard into conversation about measurement or estimation | Animal picture ... springboard into conversation about measurement. |

Stock photos of oranges and giraffe from Dollar Photo Club, www.dollarphotoclub.com/Search?k=sea& filters%5Bcontent_type%3Aphoto%5D=1&filters%5Bcontent_type%3Aillustration%5D=1&filters%5B content_type%3Avector%5D=1&search=Search. Used with permission.

21st-Century Technologies

Using 21st-century technologies is another way to launch mini-lessons. Pretsky (2001) calls the children that we teach "digital natives" and he calls us (the teachers) "digital immigrants." There is an ever-growing number of 21st-century technologies that you can use to launch mini-lessons, such as Glogster, Animoto, and Prezi. Glogster.edu is an online presentation tool that you can use in many ways. First, you can use it as an instructional strategy. There are many public glogs about math topics that you can pull and use to launch a lesson. For example, if you are teaching fourth grade, you can pull down a glog that students made about angles. In this glog, the students have put up some basic information; but they also imported a video of students acting out the vocabulary, which is invaluable. Another way to use glogs is to make your own glogs and link up pictures, games, and videos. This can take time, but then you can show it in class, and you can also post it on your class or school website so parents can see what you are discussing in class.

A different 21st-century tool is Prezi, which is a 3-D PowerPoint experience. You can play with text size and distance, and import various media into the Prezi. It is a different type of experience than PowerPoint and is more of a 21st-century tool for presenting information with students. Another 21st-century tool is Animoto. An Animoto presentation is a fast 30-second commercial-like experience that you can create for your students. It is a way to launch a topic. On the Animoto website, you can upload whatever pictures and images you want to show about the topic, and then also pick a soundtrack from the site or an imported one. Then the site rearranges the pictures in a different mini-commercial for every different showing. It is a quick, visual, 21st-century tool to introduce a topic.

Figure 5.14 3 Great 21st-Century Technologies

Three Great 21st-Century Technologies
http:// animoto.com/
http://edu.glogster.com/
www.biteslide.com/

Figure 5.15 Two Other Things Besides PowerPoint

Two Other Things Besides PowerPoint
http://prezi.com/
http://voicethread.com/

Summary

As you think about the role of mini-lessons in Math Workshop, you have to think about the frames you are using to do those mini-lessons. Although literacy offers many great ideas, you have to forge your own architecture that organically fits your discipline. In Math Workshop, the five elements of mathematical proficiency should frame your mini-lessons.

There are a variety of different formats that you can use to introduce math mini-lessons. It is your responsibility as the teacher to choose a variety of mini-lesson formats to keep your students engaged and interacting with the content. Students need to be intellectually prompted into discussions about academically rigorous content. They should be a part of the mini-lessons and understand how this foundational part of the Math Workshop works.

Key Points

Whole-group mini-lessons:

- Invite wonder
- Are teacher-led but engage your students
- Discuss (concepts, procedures, reasoning, strategy, disposition)
- Have many different formats (picture books, pictures, songs, chants, poems, discussion, videos)
- Incorporate 21st-century technologies (like Animoto, Glogster, Prezi)

Reflection Questions

1. What types of formats do you presently use for mini-lessons? Do you sometimes use 21st-century technologies as part of your mini-lesson format?
2. What types of mini-lessons do you use to build mathematical proficiency? Do you use all five? Which ones do you use the most? Which ones do you use the least?
3. What new ideas do you have about mini-lesson formats and mini-lesson types after reading this chapter?

6

Math Workstations
Meaningful Engagement

Furious activity is no substitute for understanding.

H. H. Williams

Welcome to room 102. Mrs. Johnson is facilitating Math Workstations. She has been working with her math coach to find meaningful ways to engage her first graders. It is the middle of the year and they are working on place value. She has a diverse class of students, so she has grouped them in tables so that they are challenged according to their current skill level.

At the first table, there are four children working with place value match cards. They have a set of 20 cards with ten pairs. The children are matching the place value picture represented in base-ten blocks with the numeral. At the second table, there are five children and they are working in pairs. One person rolls two dice and makes the largest number, and the other person puts base-ten blocks on the mat to represent that number. At the third table, the children are working on the computer. They are working in pairs on base-ten activities from the National Library of Virtual Manipulatives. At the fourth table, the children are spelling out their initials in base-ten blocks and tracing the blocks and counting up the value of their initials. At the fifth table, the children are using the number grid to help them find the answers to the +10 game.

Mrs. Johnson is walking around the room taking anecdotal notes on three children who she has chosen to watch for the day. She just finished a guided math group. During this lesson, she worked with the advanced-level learners and had them show different numbers in two ways. She is getting ready to give the Big Switch Signal, so that all the groups can switch from working on this first set of activities to the second set of activities. After the second set of activities, she will play the xylophone (which is her clean-up signal), so that all the children will quickly and quietly prepare to come to the rug to discuss their math work for the day. Mrs. Johnson makes a written note to herself that tomorrow she definitely wants to do a math interview with Daniel about representing tens and ones. She is thinking he might be ready to move to a more challenging group.

Defining Math Workstations

Math Workstations are differentiated, standards-based, engaging activities that foster mathematical thinking. The goal of Math Workstations is to encourage students to make sense of math by engaging in sustained practice over time that allows them to build conceptual understanding, procedural fluency, and problem solving skills. Through a variety of experiences that start at the concrete level and then scaffold through to the pictorial level and then the abstract level, children get to feel the math, see the math, and do the math. Math Workstations are based on research that states "practice should be varied, . . . incorporate multiple processes for learning and . . . be motivational" (Allsopp, Kyger & Lovin, 2007).

Math Workstations in this book are defined as the actual activities that students do. They are not a physical place in the room, although some of the activities are in fixed locations, such as the computer workstation or the interactive bulletin board. However, for the most part, they are stored in plastic bags, boxes, folders, and tubs. The children stay in their designated groups (which change by readiness, learning style, and interest level), and the table captain brings the workstations to the table.

The Goal of Math Workstations

> When I worked on my game, that's what I thought about. When it happened I set another goal, a reasonable, manageable goal that I could realistically achieve if I worked hard enough. I guess I approached it with the end in mind. I knew exactly where I wanted to go, and I focused on getting there.
> Jordan & Vancil, 1994

The goal of Math Workstations is for students to build mathematical proficiency by continuous, purposeful practice in standards-based, hands-on, academically rigorous ways that help students gain confidence and pride in their work. The more success they have doing the math, the more motivated they are to stay in the learning zone. Students like to laugh and learn by doing something that challenges them just enough, but that is still fun and engaging. Math Workstations allow children to revisit, review, practice, and be enriched so that they become flexible, confident, proficient mathematicians. Math Workstations also aim to give students practice with their peers as well as individual practice.

Getting Started

There are many ways to do Math Workstations. You can pick a concept that you would like to explore through workstations and then go from there.

Planning is the essential component to successful workstations. Remember that classroom management starts way before the class ever gets there! An effective use of instructional minutes is a pre-planned event. The first step in planning is to figure out what you want to teach. Actually, it is to figure out what you should teach. Figure out what your standards are and then create workstations that teach those standards. Second, you want to figure out what your students need to know in terms of those standards. This necessitates that you do some pre-assessment so that you can differentiate your groups by readiness levels. You will, of course, also do other methods of differentiation, but you will need to know your students' readiness levels in terms of the Big Idea that you will be exploring. We will discuss how assessment is intricately interwoven throughout the process of using workstations in Chapter 9.

Forming Differentiated Math Workstation Groups

Differentiated instruction is one of the pillars that provide the foundation for effective Math Workstations. As my mentor Coco Aguirre taught me, "If a student doesn't learn the way you teach, then teach the way they learn." This is a simple but powerful truth. Meet the children where they are and then take them to the next level. For me, differentiation is about always asking myself, "If they aren't getting it, what can I do differently?" Tomlinson (1999) speaks of how differentiated instruction results in academically responsive classrooms. In this type of classroom, teachers are aware of the academic levels of their students as well as their learning modalities and interests, and therefore they can and do create curriculum designed to respond to these needs.

In Math Workstations, children work on targeted skill sets based on their readiness, interest level, and learning styles. Teachers differentiate the content, the process and products as they design the workstations. Differentiated workstations not only directly benefit children, but they are a major component of classroom management; this is because children that are being appropriately challenged are neither frustrated from the work being too hard nor bored from the work being too easy. Children that are working in what Vygotsky (1978) calls their "zone of proximal development" are much more likely to stay on task, because they are interested and able to do the work at hand.

Sometimes, you can form groups by *readiness level*. Based on the pre-assessment, group your students together for activities that allow them to practice and improve on their current level of mathematical understanding about the topic. Let's look at Mrs. Lee's first-grade classroom:

Mrs. Lee's class is studying patterns. She has two novice-level groups who are just learning basic patterns. Mrs. Lee has the first novice-level group working on AB patterns using a Unifix Cube pattern strip. They are simply **matching** the patterns to the strip. The second novice-level group is working on AB patterns using Bear pattern strips.

The next two groups are apprentice-level groups. They are working on AB and ABC patterns. The first apprentice group is picking a Laminated pattern strip and then **labeling** the pattern with letters using a dry erase marker. The second apprentice group is **creating** ABC patterns with Bingo Dot Paints. The fifth group is the expert-level learners. They are working on **extending** ABCD patterns using Pattern Block pattern strips.

An example of a Math Workstation Board with students grouped by readiness is shown in Figure 6.1.

Figure 6.1 Math Workstations: We Are Working on Patterns

Math Workstations We Are Working on Patterns		
Day	Group	Workstation
Friday	Horses	Extend **AB** Patterns with Pattern Block Cards A B A B ? ? ?
	Tigers	Computer Pattern Games
	Giraffes	Describe Patterns on Pattern Cards with Letters **AB or ABC?**
	Elephants	Create Your OWN Patterns with Bingo Dabbers: Choose AB, AABB, ABC, ABCD
	Leopards	Practice Growing Patterns with Foam Shapes on Strips

Other times, you can form the groups by *learning style*, meaning that there is a variety of activities based on the topic that allows the children to work based on different learning modalities and intelligences. Let's take a look at Mr. Santo's class:

Mr. Santos is studying geometry with his second graders. He has set up Math Workstations differentiated by learning style. The children selected which workstations they wanted to go to at the beginning of the day by putting their picture under that workstation during morning routines. The children at Table 1 are painting and labeling shape posters. This workstation appeals to the visual spatial learners. The children at Table 2 are cutting out 3-D shapes from a magazine and categorizing them on the class mural, entitled "We See Shapes All Around Us." This workstation appeals to the logical-mathematical and visual-spatial learners. The children at Table 3 are playing with pattern block puzzles, where the task is to find several ways to fill in a picture using different blocks and then record the findings on a template. This workstation appeals to the kinesthetic, visual-spatial, and logical mathematical learners. The children at Table 4 are working with the Flip Camera, making short videos about shapes. This workstation appeals to the linguistic and digital learners. The children at Table 5 are working at an ongoing Hot Topics workstation that includes money and time. The Hot Topics workstation is a way to practice the basic skills throughout the year. The children get to choose whether they want to work on money or time. Three of the children have chosen to play with the money match puzzles up to 50 cents. The other two children have chosen to work on the time concentration game (matching analog and digital times to the hour, 1/2 hour and by 5 minutes).

See the Multiplication Workstation Chart, which gives another example of planning workstations by learning style (Figures 6.2 and 6.3).

Sometimes, you can form groups by *interest*. For example, Ms. Robinson allows her children free-choice workstations on Fridays. When the children enter the classroom in the morning, they get to choose their workstations. Each week, the tables of children get to choose their workstations in a different order. They can pick between the numbers workstation, the geometry workstation, the pattern workstation, the fact workstation, the measurement workstation, and the graphing workstation. The activities change each week, but the basic theme of each workstation stays the same.

Another way to do free-choice workstations is to have the children stay at their regular tables and then bring them three or four activities to choose from. So if they are working on shapes, Ms. Robinson might bring them: 1) a shape dot-to-dots sheet; 2) magazines to find, cut out and make a shape poster; 3) shape stencils; and 4) shapes templates to fill in with play dough.

Figure 6.2 Math Workstations Unit Planner

Math Workstations Unit Planner 5th Grade Mr. Lee			
Topic	**Pre-Assessment (At the beginning of the Chapter)**	**Math Workstations**	**I can statements**
Fluency	*Fluency*	*Addition Games* *Subtraction Games* *Multiplication Games* *Division Games*	*I can add and subtract within 20 quickly.* *I can add and subtract multi-digit numbers using efficient strategies.* *I can multiply and divide within 144 using efficient strategies.*
Word Problems	*Word Problem Test*	*Add To, Take From, Part Part, Whole, and Comparison Problems* *Equal Group, Array, and Comparison Problems*	*I can solve multi-step problems using a variety of strategies and models.*
Division	*Pre-test*	*Model with Base-Ten Blocks (Area Model)* *Model with a Tape Diagram* *Model with Equal Groups* *Model with an Open Array*	*I can divide using a variety of strategies based on place value, properties and the relationship between the operations.*

The children can then pick which activity they want to work with right there at their desk and work on it. Any of these ideas work; they all just take planning ahead. You must plan for any of these scenarios so that the workstations are organized and your "Free-Choice Day" runs smoothly. Diller (2003) talks about "controlled choice," meaning that the teacher provides children with enough activities to be excited about, but not so many that they are overwhelmed.

Figure 6.3 Multiplication Workstations

Multiplication Workstations			
Math Library: Multiplication Picture Books Writing Multiplication Stories Solving Multiplication Stories *Linguistic*	Multiplying with the Multiplication Chart *Logical-Mathematical*	Listen and Sing Along with the Various Multiplication Songs *Musical*	Making Big Multiplication Posters *Visual-Spatial*
Play Partner Board Games; Playing Popsicle Games; Play Power Towers *Interpersonal*	Playing Computer Multiplication Games *Intrapersonal/ Visual-Spatial/ Digital*	Multiplication in Real Life: Children Finding/Making Pictures of Multiplication in Real Life *Naturalistic*	Building Arrays Life-Sized Slides and Ladders Multiplication Game *Bodily-Kinesthetic*

Free Choice Is Not a Free-For-All

Choice isn't about just picking a math activity. Choice is about allowing students to participate in their own learning journey and take some ownership of, and responsibility for, the process. On choice days they get to choose what they will do, who they will do it with, how they will do it, and when it will happen. It allows them to "feel the power and control" over math that engaged learners need (Jobe & Dayton-Sakari, 1999). Choice is not just randomness. Students still are responsible for choosing activities where they can practice with purpose.

One way to make sure that your students are practicing with purpose is to have different types of activities at the workstations. The activities should always be leveled. There should be some "everybody" games, too. These are games that everybody can play. They are either a topic from the year before that all students still struggle with or definitely need practice with, or they could be topics studied earlier in the year. You can label the bags in a distinct color in all the workstations to allow your students to quickly recognize them and get started with the work.

Scheduling

The point of workstations is sustained, meaningful, standards-based practice over time. Some teachers do workstations every day as part of the student work period. Other teachers do them two or three times a week. Some teachers do them only once a week. It just depends on the school's schedule and flexibility. Ideally, you should think about doing Math Workstations at least two or three times a week, and more if possible. After the Workshop Opening, students go to their designated workstation tables, and the table leaders bring the workstations to the table. Sometimes, children do one rotation. Other times, children do two rotations. Math Workstations usually last 10–12 minutes.

Posting the Math Workshop Schedule

I suggest prominently posting the Math Workshop schedule that you're using in the classroom so that children know exactly what is happening. There are many different ways to post the workstations, including foam boards, corkboards, rotating boards, magnetic boards, chalkboards, or pocket charts. The most important element of any Math Workstation Board is to list the names of the students. There must be icons, with names and pictures of the workstation options. Some teachers use icons that have drawings, while others use photographs. Whatever system you use, you must have a way to easily rotate the tasks and the students. Pictures and words help everyone have access to the information. In the first 20 days of school, your students will learn how to read the board so they understand what it means. Oftentimes, teachers go over the Math Workstation schedule during their morning meeting routine (see Figures 6.4, 6.5, 6.6, and 6.7).

Figure 6.4 Sample Daily Schedule of Math Block, 75 Minutes

Sample Daily Schedule of Math Block, 75 Minutes		
8:30–9:45	Math Block	Activities
8:30–8:45	Daily Routines	
8:45–9:00	Whole Group	Go Over Big Ideas Teach a Specific Concept, Strategy, or Skill
9:00–9:15	Math Workstations 1st Round	Guided Math/Workstation Work
9:15–9:30	Math Workstations 2nd Round	Math Conferences/Interview Kidwatching
9:30–9:45	Share	Debrief Math with Students

Figure 6.5 Math Workstation Schedule: Week of November 17, 2014

Math Work Station Schedule
Week November 17th 2014

Rockets

Monday: Fluency, Digital, Teacher
Wednesday: Teacher, Fluency, Word Problems
Friday: Free Choice

Stars

Monday: Teacher, Fluency, Word Problems
Wednesday: Fluency, Digital, Teacher
Friday: Free Choice

Spaceships

Monday: Word Problems, Teacher, Digital
Wednesday: Digital, Teacher, Fluency
Friday: Teacher, Free Choice, Fluency

Planets

Monday: Digital, Fluency, Word Problems
Wednesday: Free Choice, Teacher, Digital
Friday: Free Choice, Teacher

Tuesday: Regular Math Program, Journal Writing, Conferences
Thursday: Regular Math Program, Journal Writing, Conferences

Figure 6.6 Weekly Workstation Plans

Weekly Workstation Plans
Content Strand: Number Sense
Grade: K
Essential Question: What is the Shape of Numbers?
Big Idea: Each Number Has a Special Way That We Write It
Resources: Poems, Books
All Group Activities Are Differentiated by Group

Groups	Monday	Tuesday	Wednesday	Thursday	Friday
Table 1	Sand Numbers/ Paint Numbers	Play Dough Numbers/ Magnet Numbers	Stencils/Jumbo Paper Number	Class Number Poster Mural/Mud Numbers	Individual Number Books or Posters. This book is created from a Class Neighborhood Number walk. Photos were taken with a digital camera. The class then created number photo essays. We used Tana Hoban's books as our Math Mentor Texts.
Table 2	Play DoughNumbers/ Magnet Numbers	Stencils/Jumbo Paper Number	Class Number Poster Mural/Mud Numbers	Sand Numbers/ Paint Numbers	
Table 3	Stencils/Jumbo Paper Number	Class Number Poster Mural/ Mud Numbers	Sand Numbers/ Paint Numbers	Play Dough Numbers/ Magnet Numbers	
Table 4	Class Number Poster Mural/Mud Numbers	Sand Numbers/ Paint Numbers	Play Dough Numbers/ Magnet Numbers	Stencils/Jumbo Paper Number	

Figure 6.7 Weekly Math Workstation Plans

Weekly Math Workstation Plans
Content Strand: Fractions
Grade: 4
Essential Question: How Do We Use Fractions in Our Everyday Lives?
Big Idea: Fractions Are Everywhere
Resources: Poems, Books, Websites, Activities

Groups	Monday	Tuesday	Wednesday	Thursday	Friday
Table 1 Novice	Math Program Lessons	Equivalent Fractions with Fraction Circles/Squares	Math Program Lessons	Equivalent Fractions Strip Flipbook Denominators 1, 2, 3, 4, 6, 8	Whole Class: Math Fraction Tic-Tac-Toe Math Fraction Tracks
Table 2 Novice		Equivalent Fraction Strip Flipbook 1, 2, 3, 4, 6, 8		Equivalent Fractions with Fraction Circles/Squares	
Table 3 Apprentice		Equivalent Fraction Poster		Equivalent Fraction Flipbook 1, 2, 3, 4, 5, 6, 8, 9, 10	
Table 4 Apprentice		Equivalent Fraction Flipbook 1, 2, 3, 4, 5, 6, 8, 9, 10		Equivalent Fraction Poster	
Table 5 Expert		Equivalent Fraction Game		Equivalent Fraction Flipbook with Circles	

Math mini-lessons are poems and picture books and pictures that teach about fractions during this week.

Introducing the Children to Math Workstations

Workstations help children practice what they have been introduced to during other instructional times and extend their learning. Spend time introducing you workstations and talking about their purpose. Make sure your students understand why they are doing them and follow up with anchor charts (see Figures 6.8 and 6.9). It is very important that children have had previous experiences with the workstation activities and that they are comfortable working with them. During whole-class instruction,

Figure 6.8 Anchor Chart: Math Workstations

Math Workstations		
Looks Like	Sounds Like	Feels Like
• Working alone • Working with partners • Working with groups • Staying on task • Waiting your turn • Helping each other • Using the toolkits	• Using inside voices • Saying "Please" and "Thank You" • Saying "You can do it!" • Using math words • Stating how the game helps you learn • Fun	• Great • Encouraging • Happy

Figure 6.9 Anchor Chart: Workstation Expectations

Workstation Expectations	What Are Math Workstations?
Get started right away. Use your inside voices. Stay with your group. Share stuff! Use the tools. Talk nice. Be happy. Respect each other. Clean up. Do the math!	Spaces to practice what we know and get better: • Fluency • Digital • Vocabulary • Word problems • Unit workstations

for example, I often play the games with the class by dividing the class into teams to ensure that the children are very familiar with the games. At other times, I introduce the new workstations in small guided math groups. Sometimes this is the best way to introduce an activity to the children; since the activities are differentiated, the teacher can focus on targeted skill sets with each group.

The Location and Management of the Workstations

In this book, most of the Math Workstations are moveable workstations located in tubs, jumbo plastic bags, magazine holders, or baskets. These containers are located in the Math Workstation storage area in the classroom. I only put the current workstations in the area, as it would be overwhelming and cumbersome to have all the workstations for the year out at once. The workstations are clearly labeled. When it is workstation time, the designated workstation leader for the week takes the station containers to their existing table or grouping of desks, which becomes the actual space where the students work.

Workstation bags have everything that is needed for that workstation inside of them. For example, the dice, dominos, or cards are placed inside a snack-sized baggie and the snap cubes, pattern blocks, or beans go in a different sized baggie. All these baggies go inside the workstation container. It is crucial that there are enough materials inside each workstation. For example, if the students are doing place value pictures, then there needs to be enough pre-cut hundreds, tens, and ones so that everybody has enough. I usually cut anything that needs to be cut ahead of time (or get parent volunteers to do it), because I don't want the students spending the period cutting instead of doing the math. I make sure that whatever we need for that workstation is in the container; if, for example, they need glue or paper, I put it in there. The game recording sheets are inside the workstation folder, which is also in the workstation container. Inside each of the workstation containers is a detailed Task Card with pictures and instructions. This is very important so that children have a model to reference.

While most of the workstations are traveling workstations (portable), some are stationary (permanent). For example, the math big book station usually takes place at the big book easel. The math computer game station takes place at the computers. The interactive bulletin board workstations take place at the actual bulletin board.

Teacher During Math Workstations

As the teacher, you will do a variety of activities during Math Workstation time. Some of the time, you will be kidwatching. You can keep a clipboard with sticky notes and try to make two or three written observations a day. Sometimes you will even sit down with a group of the children and watch them play a game, asking probing questions and noting their thinking. Other times, you may pull a child and engage in an informal conversation or do a more formal interview. You will spend two to four days pulling a guided math group; throughout the week, you will pull different groups from various levels. You should connect with all the groups, not just the lowest level or the highest level.

Students During Workstation Time

During Math Workstations, students either work alone, with partners, or with groups. Oftentimes when students are working alone, they are in a group doing it. It is similar to parallel play where children are playing together but each is doing his or her own thing. For example, a group of students might be working in the fluency workstation, with each student practicing with the student's own set of fluency cards (see Figure 6.11). In the fluency workstation, students might play a game with a partner like addition or subtraction war, where they roll a double dice, add the dots together, and the person with the highest sum wins that roll and earns that many points. After five rounds, the person with the most points wins. In the same workstation, students can play group games, including board, dice, and domino games (see Figures 6.10, 6.12, and 6.13).

Figure 6.10 Tips for Playing Games

Tips for Playing Games:

1. Have the students play in rounds of 4 or 5, because it keeps them engaged.
2. Have the students record their thinking on some sort of recording sheet.
3. Have a variety of games that give students the opportunity to practice the same skill over time.

Figure 6.11 Fluency Cards

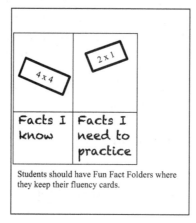

Students should have Fun Fact Folders where they keep their fluency cards.

Figure 6.12 Using Double Dice

Students love
double dice!
They are colorful
and full of
possibilities.

Figure 6.13 Ways I Can Work in Math Workstations

Ways I Can Work in Math Workstations		
I can play by myself. This is an example of a math problem solving work board that students work with by themselves. It is self checking. 	I can play with a partner. Card, dice and domino games with recording sheets are great for partner work. 	I can play with a group. There should be several different board games in the workstations so that students can play partner and group games. 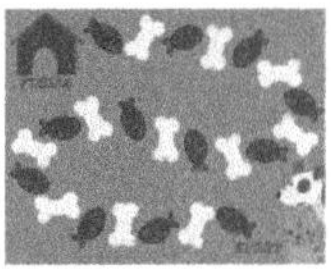

Teachers will often put up *I can* statements to remind students of the different types of things they can do at the station (Diller, 2003) (see Figure 6.14). When students have several options at the workstation, they are less likely to get bored (see Figure 6.15). When they tire of playing one game, they can close it up and open up another one. Students can only actually switch to a new workstation when it is time to switch. On free-choice days, they go wherever they want. On the other days, they are scheduled to go to specific workstations.

Kristin from the One Stop Teacher Shop puts her workstations in colorfully decorated tennis ball cans and puts different activities written on paper inside the "I can" cans (www.onestopteachershop.com/2014/04/making-test-prep-funseriously.html). Then, as the students do the activities, they keep track on a piece of paper all the "I can" tasks that they have done throughout the unit. This is a brilliant idea and quite motivating for the students.

Figure 6.14 In the Fluency Station

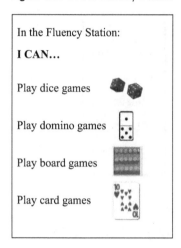

In the Fluency Station:

I CAN...

Play dice games

Play domino games

Play board games

Play card games

The Importance of Why: **I Can** *Statements*

Students should know what the math is and how they are practicing it at the workstation. Students should be able to explain, "I am practicing my doubles facts with this board game. Doubles helps us to add faster." Every workstation should have the *I can* statements written on them. Students should be able to name the math they are practicing and understand how the activity they are doing helps them to learn. Also, it is helpful if they think about where they are in terms of mastering the topic. Marzano (2006) has written a great deal about this with his four levels of understanding.

Keeping Students a Part of the Goal Setting Process

Students should know exactly what they are working on in the workstation. There should be *I can* statements written in the station. I like the idea of tracking sheets that state the *I can* statement and the goal that the students are working on all together. This helps students to set goals: "reasonable, manageable" steps that they can achieve if they focus and work hard in their stations. Like Michael Jordan, they need to approach the work with the end in mind.

Let's look at two examples of framing the work around *I can* statements. One example is using the addition fact table so that students can keep track of their learning of the basic facts. As students learn each set of facts, they color it in. The table is color-coded by strategies; for example, all of the zero facts might be orange, and all the +1 facts might be green. In this way, students can see and celebrate what they have learned, and still view the landscape ahead of them. When students come to the workstation, they can play any of the games they know and they can also play the color they are working on. The set of facts that they are working on should be outlined in some sort of way or have an asterisk by them. You could have two asterisks by the facts a student has learned and one asterisk by the current set

Figure 6.15 Math Workstation Ideas

Math Workstation Ideas			
Fluency	**Word Problems**	**Digital**	**Vocabulary/Writing**
• Board Games • Card Games • Power Towers (cups) • Dice Games • Domino Games • Popsicle Games	• Solving Word Problems • Writing Word Problems • Sorting Word Problems • Matching Problems with the Equation and/or Models • Use Templates in the Beginning • Use Rubrics • Use Thinking Blocks to Teach Tape Diagramming of Word Problems	• Games (fluency, word problems, and math concepts) • Photo Essays • VoiceThread (a great web program where students/teachers can put up pictures/PowerPoints and then everyone else can make comments) • Glogster (another great web tool to create visual presentation boards about topics) Great to set up and have students use in a workstation or for older students to have them make glogs about different math topics	• Math Vocabulary Tic-Tac-Toe • Math Word Finds & Define • Math Crossword Puzzles • Math Concentration • Math Bingo • Class Big Books • Interactive Journals • Graphic Organizers
	Give the students a word problem test to make sure they are working on problems in their zone of proximal development. Separate the different word problem types into different envelopes. Have students work on the type they are trying to master. The levels are in a hierarchy, so, for example, students shouldn't be working on multiplicative comparison problems until they know how to solve additive comparison problems.	Try to integrate at least one 21st-century technology into your instructional program. 5 Great Websites: *Math Play* *Math Playground* *Illuminations* *Harvey's Homepage (for SMART Board)* *Johnnies Homepage*	It is important to have students write about math and use math vocabulary on a continuous basis. *Keystone Math Vocabulary* (www.aea1.k12.ia.us/en/curriculum_instruction_and_assessment/math/english_language_learner_supports/math_vocabulary/) has great graphic organizers. *Granite School District* (www.graniteschools.org/mathvocabulary/) has great vocabulary words for all grade levels.

Figure 6.16 Chart for Keeping Track of Learning

| Plus 0 | Plus 1, 2, 3 | Doubles | Make 10 | Doubles +1 | Doubles −1 |

| Doubles +2 | Doubles −2 | Lucky 7, 8, 9 (Always make it a ten) | Plus 10 |

	0	1	2	3	4	5	6	7	8	9	10
0	0 + 0	0 + 1	0 + 2	0 + 3	0 + 4	0 + 5	0 + 6	0 + 7	0 + 8	0 + 9	0 + 10
1	1 + 0	1 + 1	1 + 2	1 + 3	1 + 4	1 + 5	1 + 6	1 + 7	1 + 8	1 + 9	1 + 10
2	2 + 0	2 + 1	2 + 2	2 + 3	2 + 4	2 + 5	2 + 6	2 + 7	2 + 8	2 + 9	2 + 10
3	3 + 0	3 + 1	3 + 2	3 + 3	3 + 4	3 + 5	3 + 6	3 + 7	3 + 8	3 + 9	3 + 10
4	4 + 0	4 + 1	4 + 2	4 + 3	4 + 4	4 + 5	4 + 6	4 + 7	4 + 8	4 + 9	4 + 10
5	5 + 0	5 + 1	5 + 2	5 + 3	5 + 4	5 + 5	5 + 6	5 + 7	5 + 8	5 + 9	5 + 10
6	6 + 0	6 + 1	6 + 2	6 + 3	6 + 4	6 + 5	6 + 6	6 + 7	6 + 8	6 + 9	6 + 10
7	7 + 0	7 + 1	7 + 2	7 + 3	7 + 4	7 + 5	7 + 6	7 + 7	7 + 8	7 + 9	7 + 10
8	8 + 0	8 + 1	8 + 2	8 + 3	8 + 4	8 + 5	8 + 6	8 + 7	8 + 8	8 + 9	8 + 10
9	9 + 0	9 + 1	9 + 2	9 + 3	9 + 4	9 + 5	9 + 6	9 + 7	9 + 8	9 + 9	9 + 10
10	10 + 0	10 + 1	10 + 2	10 + 3	10 + 4	10 + 5	10 + 6	10 + 7	10 + 8	10 + 9	10 + 10

of facts the student is working on presently. The other facts that have yet to be learned are left without any markings (see Figure 6.16).

Another way of keeping your students accountable to the learning goals is to have them use a tracker sheet of the workstation activities that they have done in that unit. As the students work through the workstations, they date it and color in that square. They have to either write a reflection or attach an artifact sheet to the workstation accountability template. For example, a fourth-grade class working on fractions might have a sheet like the one in Figure 6.17.

Keeping Children Accountable

It is really important to have structures in place to hold the children accountable for their work. Each student has a workstation notebook where he or she records designated work. Each student also has a workstation folder with two sides. One side is for completed work (i.e., game recording sheets), and the other side is for work in progress (i.e., storytelling sheets).

Figure 6.17 Reflection Sheet for Fraction Work

We are working on fractions.		
I can make and explain equivalent fractions using visual models.	**I can recognize equivalent fractions.**	**I can generate equivalent fractions using numbers.**
Make equivalent fractions with pattern blocks (use pattern block mats).	I can recognize equivalent fractions in sets. (Concentration Match Game)	Use model/number mats (concrete).
Make equivalent fractions with fraction circles (use birthday cake game).	I can recognize equivalent fractions (practice with video games).	Use picture/number mats (pictorial).

They keep these notebooks and folders in a Workstation Time Tub that is located in the same area where the workstations are stored. Some teachers elect to have the children keep the folders and notebooks in their desks.

You should check these folders periodically throughout the week. Some teachers will go through all of them on Friday to review the work and then use them to further assess the students. For example, by looking at the kindergarten number-writing artifact sheets and seeing who is still having trouble with reversals, you can then create specific interventions for those students. Sometimes, when conferencing with a student, you can look at the student's workstation folder and discuss the work. The folders are also used during parent conferences to discuss work.

There are different types of activity sheets that students can record their work on. There is a difference between activity sheets and worksheets. Never use worksheets. They are a one-shot deal, and oftentimes they don't require much thinking. On the other hand, activity sheets will allow you to differentiate, your students to think, and everyone to have fun (see Figure 6.18).

Rules About the Math Workstation Stuff
Sometimes, the littlest things can threaten to derail your Math Workshop (see Figures 6.19 and 6.20). Let's start with glue. Students have to learn the glue rules. There is a great book called, *Too Much Glue* by Jason Lefebvre. This is a great book to jumpstart the conversation about using glue appropriately. Many teachers use poems and songs to reinforce glue protocols. There is a woman named Mrs. Miner who actually takes her students through a super-duper glue course and then gives them an actual license to glue. This is hilarious! The license and description can be found for free on her website (www.mrsminersmonkeybusiness.com/2011/11/heres-license-to-glue-freebie.html).

Figure 6.18 Scaffolded Activity Sheets

Scaffolded Activity Sheets			
This activity sheet is scaffolded. Students must roll the dice and do a drawing to scaffold their adding.	This activity sheet is not scaffolded. Students must roll the dice and add with just the numbers.	This activity sheet is a variation on the roll and show it is a pull and show. Keep students interested by varying the manipulatives.	This game is the least scaffold. It is quite engaging. Students choose 3 numbers as quickly as they can and add them together. It is choice and student led. Watch the numbers that the students pick.

For dice activities, have the students roll the dice in some sort of open container with foam or felt at the bottom to soften the noise level. When your students are using double dice, have them roll the dice in the container with felt or foam to soften the noise level.

Noisy Spaces, Playing Places!

Classes with children working together can become very noisy! It is important to distinguish between productive noise and chaotic noise. However, there can be productive chaos! The most important thing is that students are on task. There are many ways to manage the noise. Noise management has to begin when you introduce the workstations. Practice with your students how they are supposed to behave during workstation time. Have them work in cooperative groups, so there are designated people for getting materials, cleaning up, and getting the teacher. It is a good idea to keep a noise monitor (see Figure 3.11) somewhere in the front of the room, so if the students get too noisy, you have a way of telling them without yelling over them!

Figure 6.19 Rules for Scissors and Dice

Scissor Rules	Dice
Careful, Careful Take your time Safety first, yours and mine!	Roll, roll Really calm Calmly as can be, Keep the dice on the table for everyone to see! (to the tune of Row Row Row Your Boat)

Figure 6.20 Rules for Glue

Glue Rules:	Glue Rules:
Dot, Dot, Dot Not Alot! Clean it up, Twist it tight! Put it back, Nice and right!	Out to Glue In when done Twist cap tight Back on right!

When working with the different numeracy activities, students will sometimes work alone and other times they will work with a partner. It is important to remember that some students prefer to work alone (intrapersonal meaning making), while others enjoy working with others (interpersonal meaning making). The stations are taken to a work area by the table leader, and the children at the tables work either independently, in pairs, or sometimes as a whole group. There are usually no more than four or five students working together in a group at a time.

Weekly Workstation Reflections
Individual Reflections
It is important that your students get a chance to reflect on the work they are doing in Math Workstations. There are different ways to do this. One way is to do an oral check-in during the Share, with a simple thumbs-up

Figure 6.21 Math Workstation Reflection Sheet

Math Workstation Reflection Sheet

Name: _____

Date: _____

How I did	I did great!  I rock! I worked well with team members. I did all my work. I tried hard.	I did ok! I did ok. I could try harder. I did most of my work. I kinda got along with everyone.	I need to do better.  I need to work harder. I didn't get along with others. I didn't finish my work. I didn't try very hard.
Monday			
Tuesday			
Wednesday			
Thursday			
Friday			
Overall this week!			

and thumbs-down self-reflection. The question could be something like, "Give yourself a thumbs-up if you really worked hard in workstations today, a thumbs-sideways if you kinda worked but played a little, and thumbs-down if you didn't do what you were supposed to do. Now turn and talk to your neighbor about your reflection." Other times, the students can vote with a happy face or an Oh-oooo face on a popsicle stick. Still other times, they can reflect in their journals about the work they are doing (see Figure 6.21).

Group Reflections
It is important to have your students reflect on their work in groups (Johnson, Johnson & Smith, 1998; Kagan, 2009). The big idea is that students need to reflect on how their group work is going. They need time to write

and talk about the teamwork and the task work. There are many ways to do it. Sometimes, you can just ask a simple question such as, "How did we work in our groups today?" Students can either respond on a form, in their journal, or in a group folder. There are a variety of different types of forms to do this reflection (see Figures 6.22 and 6.23).

Figure 6.22 Our Group Reflection Sheet

Our Group Reflection Sheet

Group Members:

Date:

Project:

How we did on the fraction poster.	
We worked really hard.	
We worked well together.	
Overall, we give ourselves a	
Comments:	

Figure 6.23 Our Group Reflection Sheet: Alternate Format

Our Group Reflection

Members:
This week we did really well.
We need to work on . . .
We give ourselves a 5 4 3 2 1.

Summary

Math Workstations provide plenty of opportunities for power practice that helps students understand the math they are doing. Clements and Sarama (2009, p. 329) noted that "the importance of well-planned, free-choice play, appropriate to the ages of the children, should not be underestimated. Such play . . . if mathematized contributes to mathematics learning." When children understand math, they want to do it. It is important that you spend the time making sure that math makes sense to your students so that they can become competent, flexible, confident mathematicians. Scaffolded, differentiated learning opportunities provide plenty of opportunities to practice conceptual understanding, procedural knowledge, and problem solving skills. Successful workstations start before the children get there. They require assessing the students, creating flexible groups, and ongoing facilitation of thought-provoking activities. All teachers have the responsibility to create "intellectual environments where serious mathematical thinking is the norm" (National Council of Teachers of Mathematics, 2002).

Key Points

- Workstations should be engaging, purposeful, academically rigorous, and standards based
- Furious activity does not equal purposeful activity
- Get started with data
- Differentiate stations by readiness, choice, and learning styles
- Free choice is not a free-for-all
- Post the schedule
- Establish and reinforce workstation expectations from the beginning
- Visit the workstations weekly
- Student goals/*I Can* statements should be embedded in the station work
- Students should do artifacts or reflections for the workstation work
- Scaffold artifact sheets
- Have students reflect on workstations weekly

Reflection Questions

1. What are some current ways that you engage your students in sustained practice to develop conceptual understanding, procedural fluency, and problem solving skills? How might you expand that in new ways based on this chapter?

2. In what ways do you currently differentiate your students' math learning? How might you expand that in new ways based on this chapter?
3. How do you hold students accountable to the work they are doing in Math Workstations?

7

Guided Math Groups

Overview

One of the most important elements of Math Workshop is guided math groups. Guided math groups are small, intentional lessons with students around a particular topic. These lessons take place for 8–15 minutes, and you must always be ever-conscious of your students' attention span (which is their age plus a few minutes). A guided math lesson is short, to the point, and important. It is always in the students' zone of proximal development and is usually done in a cycle of three or four rounds to teach an idea.

Why?

Guided math groups allow your students an opportunity to talk with each other and do math. That really is the essence of the guided math group—talk and work. You will set this all in motion. You will create these multi-level experiences where students do math with understanding. If you teach everyone at the same time, then only a few of your students will learn anything meaningful; so the promise of the guided math teaching structure is that more of your students will learn more things at any given time in a unit of study.

Which Lessons?

You can't do a guided math lesson on every lesson in the year. Choose wisely. Choose the priority standards. Some of the lessons that you will do are the prerequisite gap-filling lessons. Some of the lessons will be the topics you talked about that day in the mini-lesson. Some of the lessons will be extension/enrichment lessons. Some lessons will be about fluency or word problems. The lesson you choose will depend on which group you are meeting with at the time.

Who?

Every student should work in a small guided math group sometime during each week. The National Math Report (National Mathematics Advisory Panel, 2008) said that the students that are falling through the cracks are the expert-level students, because nobody pays attention to them. Meet with every student, every week. You might meet with the struggling learners more often, but you must meet with everyone.

Your small guided math groups should be very specific. There are four levels—expert, practitioner, apprentice, and novice. The experts are above grade level. Their lessons are always an extension of the big ideas. You might be expanding the idea horizontally or vertically. Horizontally is going deeper but staying on the grade. Vertically is going into the next grade. The practitioners are on grade level. They are ready for the concepts, and they understand what is happening. They just need to practice and get really strong with the ideas. The apprentices are almost there. Apprentices somewhat understand. They always get a partially correct answer. Apprentices need some help. The novices do not know what is happening. They need a great deal of scaffolding. Too often we collapse these groups of students, but they really are distinct.

Where?

Guided math lessons can take place anywhere. Oftentimes you can designate a place in your classroom, like the kidney table, for these lessons; however, the lessons don't always have to take place there. They can take place with a small group at their workstation. Sometimes, they might take place at the interactive board or at the computer station. They can take place on the rug. Guided math lessons take place where they best make sense given the lesson.

What?

There are many different types of guided math lessons. Some lessons teach a concept. Others teach a strategy or a model. Still others focus on math talk and explanation. The chart in Figure 7.1 explains these different types of lessons.

Framework of a Guided Math Lesson

In the beginning of the guided math lesson, you should tell your students why they are there, what the math is, how it connects to the *I can* statements, and how they are going to practice it. Then, the students do the math. At the end, you should always facilitate a discussion about what the students did in the guided math group.

Figure 7.1 Types of Guided Math Lessons

Types of Guided Math Lessons		
Type	**Definition**	**Examples**
Concept	A lesson that explores a concept. The purpose of the lesson is to build conceptual understanding.	What is subtraction? What is multiplying a fraction by a fraction? What is a start unknown problem?
Procedure	A lesson that explores how to do a mathematical procedure. The purpose of the lesson is to build procedural knowledge.	How do you multiply a double-digit number by a double-digit number? How do you multiply a whole number by a fraction?
Strategy	A lesson that teaches a mathematical strategy. The purpose of the lesson is to teach students how to effectively use strategies.	How do you use compensation to add numbers with 9? How do you use the doubling/halving strategy to multiply some two-digit numbers?
Model	A lesson that teaches a mathematical model. The purpose of the lesson is to teach students how to effectively model their thinking.	How do you make and use the open number line? How do you make and use an open array?
Reasoning	A lesson that teaches students to reason out loud. The purpose of the lesson is to teach students how to think about and work with numbers flexibly.	How do you contextualize a problem? How do you decontextualize a problem? How do you reason about quantities?
Math Talk	A lesson that teaches students to talk about math. The purpose of the lesson is to teach students how to not only talk about their work, but also to talk about the work of others with each other.	How do you explain what you are thinking? How do you "friendly" disagree with somebody?

Architecture of a Lesson

- Introduction
- Student activity
- Debriefing
- Next steps.

A Framework for Understanding—Concrete, Pictorial, Abstract

The framework of a guided math lesson is simple: concrete, pictorial, and then abstract. Let's take a look (see also Figures 7.2, 7.3, 7.4, and 7.5):

A First-Grade Plan
Small Group Lesson Plan
Unit of Study: Doubles + 1 Facts
Week of: _____
Group:

Fourth-Grade Guided Math Lesson

A Fourth-Grade Plan
Small Group Lesson Plan
Unit of Study: Multiplying a Fraction by a Whole Number
Week of: _____
Group:

Figure 7.2 Framework Example for Grade 1

Monday: Introduction to Doubles
Teaching Point: Building **conceptual understanding** of number relationships
Materials: Double ten frames and counters
Do the Math: Explore number relationships counters
    For example: Let's roll a number and then build the doubles + 2 fact.
    Students use the number cubes to roll and build the fact with cubes.

$$\begin{array}{r} 5 \\ + \underline{3} \\ 8 \end{array}$$

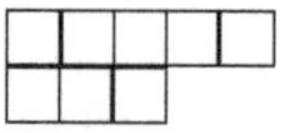

Notes:

Figure 7.3 Another Framework Example for Grade 1

Wednesday: Introduction to Doubles +2 Facts
Teaching Point: Building **pictorial understanding/abstract understanding** of number relationships
Materials: Doubles + 2 match fact with model
Do the Math: Build doubles +1 facts on the ten frame/alongside the fact

$$\begin{array}{l} 6 = 4 + 2 \\ \underline{+4} = 4 \end{array}$$

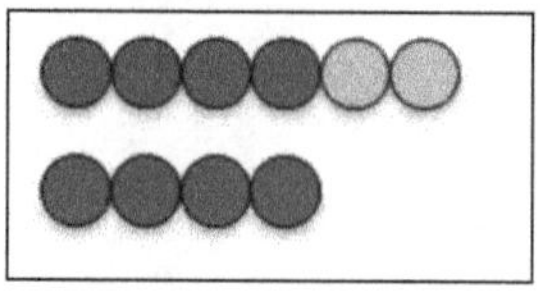

Notes:

Figure 7.4 Framework Example for Grade 4

Monday: Introduction to Multiplying a Fraction and a Whole Number
Teaching Point: Building **a concrete understanding** of number relationships
Materials: Pattern Blocks
Do the Math: Students will explore what it means to multiply a fraction by a whole number with concrete materials

$3 \times 1/3$
1. Tell a story
2. Act out the story with pattern blocks
3. Discuss the math

Set-up: 3 cakes (hexagons) 1/3s blue rhombi

Claire went to the bakery. She bought a 1/3 of the strawberry pie, a 1/3 of the apple pie, and a 1/3 of the peach pie. She bought 3 groups of a 1/3. How much pie did she buy altogether?

$1/3 + 1/3 + 1/3 = 3 \times 1/3 = 3$

Answer: 3 pieces of pie or the equivalent of whole pie

Notes:

Figure 7.5 Another Framework Example for Grade 4

Wednesday: Introduction to multiplying a whole number by a fraction
Teaching Point: Building **a concrete understanding** of number relationships.
Focus today is to talk about the difference in real situations between $3 \times 1/3$ and $1/3 \times 3$.
Materials: Pattern Blocks
Do the Math: Students will explore what it means to multiply a fraction by a whole number with concrete materials.

$1/3 \times 3$
1. Tell a story
2. Act out the story with pattern blocks
3. Discuss the math

Set-up: Pattern blocks

Grandma Betsy made 3 cakes. She gave 1/3 of the 3 cakes to her neighbor. How many cakes did she give to her neighbor?

Answer: 1 whole pie

Notes:

Figure 7.6 Three-Cycle Lesson Framework

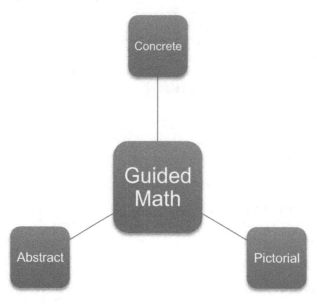

In guided math groups, your students get to do math every time. They get to use different materials than they use at other times. They always go through at least a three-cycle lesson framework of concrete, pictorial, and then abstract (meaning they meet about the topic at least three times); see Figure 7.6. You always have to think about the concrete piece of this concept. Most textbooks jump right in . . . and then teach the concept in two days. Well, all teachers know that their students can't fully understand doubles in two days. Students need time and experiences. You must look at your lessons and think about each lesson's prequel. Even *Star Wars* had a prequel! Look at your lessons and think, "Now what are the students assuming? What are the students supposed to fully understand? What part of the conversation are we walking in on? How do we catch everyone up to the current conversation?" That's where the guided math groups come in!

Doing the Math

At least 85% of the time in a guided math group, your students should be doing math: hands-on, minds-on activities where they are exploring the concepts. They should be acting things out, using objects, using drawings, and using diagrams. For example, your students might have a problem that says Chef Jamal made a cake. He added 1/3 cup of water and 1/2 cup of oil. How much liquid did he use? Your students should actually act that out with liquid before they start drawing and computing.

Questions

The right questions are so important throughout the lesson. You should plan questions for the lesson ahead of time and write them down so your students remember them. There are many different types of questions. There are content questions and there are process questions. For example, "Can you tell me exactly how you did that?" is different from "Can you explain what Joe just said?" One is a question that asks about a procedure, and the other is a question that asks about a practice (listening to and understanding the arguments of others).

Prompts/Scaffolds

Throughout the guided math lesson, your role is to prompt and scaffold. Now, there is a fine line between scaffolding and over-scaffolding. Scaffolding and prompting is important. For example, if your students are playing an addition strategy board game where they have to name the strategy they are using to add two-digit numbers, then you can listen to the strategies and prompt your students to use more efficient ones. So if Maria says, "I added 75 + 8 by counting up," you can then say, "Well, that is one strategy. Can you think of another strategy? Is there a strategy that we use often with 8s?" Now hopefully, Maria can thumb through her strategy chart or map (her personal survival guide) or look up and see a strategy poster to scaffold her thinking. Then Maria says, "Oh, I could make the 8 a 10 and the 75 a 73 and add 73 and 10 to get 83." So, your prompting is an example of scaffolding.

Here is another example. Toby says that he doesn't know how to solve 4/5 – 2/10. If you say, "Toby, take out your toolkit and think about what tool might help you solve that," then you have given Toby a prompt, a small scaffold for thinking. But if you say, "Toby, take out the two-tenths fraction circles and four-fifths and then decide what to do," you have over-scaffolded the lesson. Always let your students do the thinking. Don't think for them.

Importance of Planning

Always have a written plan (see Figures 7.7 and 7.8). It is the only way to get an overview of what is happening.

Guided Math Groups Unit _____

Week of _____ *Focus*

Figure 7.7 Written Plan

Novice	Apprentice
Lesson 1: I can round to the nearest ten with rounding mats. Concrete Pictorial Abstract Materials: rounding mats Evidence of understanding: explanation **Lesson 2:** I can round to the nearest ten with number grid. Concrete Pictorial Abstract Materials: number grids Evidence of understanding: grid	**Lesson 1:** I can round to the nearest ten with the rounding mats. Concrete Pictorial Abstract Materials: rounding mats Evidence of understanding: explanation **Lesson 2:** I can round to the nearest ten with number line. Concrete Pictorial Abstract Materials: number lines Evidence of understanding: number line
Practitioner	Expert
Lesson 1: I can round to the nearest ten with 10 grid and number line. Concrete Pictorial Abstract Materials: Evidence of understanding: number grids and lines **Lesson 2:** I can round to the nearest hundred with 1000 grid and open number line. Concrete Pictorial Abstract Materials: grids and paper Evidence of understanding: work on grids and lines	**Lesson 1:** I can nearest the nearest 10 and 100 with open number line. Concrete Pictorial Abstract Materials: paper Evidence of understanding: work on number line **Lesson 2:** I can round just by looking at numbers. Concrete Pictorial Abstract Materials: recording sheets Evidence of understanding: recording sheets

Figure 7.8 Guided Math Lessons Ideas

If a student . . .	Then you teach . . .
Doesn't know basic facts	• Scaffold the facts • Teach the fact sequence • Play specific fact board games • Play with scaffolded flash cards • Use basic fact individual rings • Play fast-fact games • Play accuracy games (dice, cards, dominos) • Do fact sorts • Practice basic fact concentration
Doesn't know math strategies	• Have students make strategy mats • Post strategy posters around the room • Reinforce strategies through games
Doesn't know how to solve word problems	• Teach the word problem hierarchy • Use various models and tools to teach problem solving • Do word problem sorts
Doesn't know how to express his or her thinking	• Scaffold the talk • Teach the talk moves • Give individual pupil talking sticks and prompts
Doesn't know how to model his or her thinking	• Teach specific models • Make and hang posters of various models • Have students keep track of models of their thinking

Summary

Guided math is an important component of Math Workshop. All students should meet in guided math groups and participate in lessons that grow their knowledge base. There are many different types of guided math lessons—some to remediate, some to practice grade level skills and some to enrich. In guided math groups, students mainly do math. Another important element of guided math lessons is having your students talk about the math they are doing. There should always be a part of the lesson where your students talk about mathematics and listen to each other. They should be held accountable for listening to each other through various questioning structures. In a guided math group, your students should be getting the individual attention that they can't get in the whole group. Keep the groups small and the learning hands-on.

Key Points

- Short, precise, intentional lessons
- Differentiated lessons
- Four levels—novice, apprentice, practitioner, expert
- Students do math
- Different types of lessons—concrete, procedural, strategic, model, reasoning, math talk

Reflection Questions

1. How often do you pull small guided math groups? Who do you pull? Why do you pull them? What are you hoping to get out of it?
2. What percentage of the time spent in your groups is hands-on? Do you always devote some time to student talk?
3. How often do you specifically plan for the cycle of engagement: concrete, pictorial, and abstract?

8

The Share

The Share is an important part of Math Workshop. It is not just a mopping up period, done in a rush, without planning or thought. The Share takes just as much planning and preparation as the other parts of an effective and productive Math Workshop. The purpose of the Share is to facilitate a conversation about math based on what has happened that day, throughout that unit, and more generally throughout the year. You are the lead facilitator, ensuring that the mathematical talk facilitates student thinking, summarizing, representing, and concretizing the math being studied. The students also lead some of the discussion and actively participate throughout the Share. Your students should have an opportunity to do some self-reflection, some partner reflection, and some group reflection.

After the student activity period, it is time for your students to gather at the rug again to discuss the activities of the day. The purpose of the Share is to do several things: concretize the learning from the day, summarize the key points in the unit thus far, take a temperature of the class to see where everybody is, possibly do some writing together and share mathematical discoveries.

There are generally three components of the Share. The first component is to recap the big ideas that your students are studying. During this component, you should review the *I can* statements associated with the current unit of study. You need to be able to tie together the *I can* statements that your students are working towards. There should be a very intentional conversation about the *I can* statements.

The second component is to do an interactive journal with your students as a class, recording the different activities and ideas that they have about the topic based on their work as a class, in guided math groups, and in their workstations. Sometimes, part of this component is to give your students a question to focus on. The students gather on the rug to listen to and/or read the focus question/s. The focus questions can be about the learning of the day, the learning of the unit, or some general learning throughout the year.

The third component is to give your students the opportunity to sit in the Share chair and talk about what they personally have been doing and learning in their workstations. This is time for your students to talk about their math goals and how they are meeting them. It is also a time for celebration! After the students share, applauding is definitely in order.

Component 1: Reflecting on the *I Can* Statements

The *I can* statements are an important part of any unit of study. They help your students to know where they are headed. They are like a learning map. You should post the *I can* statements for every unit of study at the beginning of the unit so that your students know what they are supposed to be learning (see Figure 8.1). Every day during the Share, review these statements with an emphasis on what your students have learned as well as what they are currently working on. Then have your students reflect on whether they feel like they can do that particular skill or not. For example, here is a list of *I can* statements for a unit of study in first grade on adding within 10.

Figure 8.1 Unit 5: Addition *I Can* Statements

Unit 5: Addition

I can add numbers within 10.
I can add zero facts.
I can add +1 facts.
I know my doubles within 10.
I know all my complements of 10.
I can add with different models, including the number line, the ten frame, the rekenrek, the number ladder, and counters.

During the discussion, you should reference these statements.

Mrs. Harris: This week we have been working on our +1 facts. Who can give me some examples of practicing this skill in Math Workshop?

Carlos: Today I was in the flashcard center and we were sorting all the +1 facts.

Miguel: I also sorted +1 facts with the dominos.

Kelly: "Well, me and Josie were playing +1 power towers.

Mrs. Harris: Well, all of you practiced the +1 facts, but in different ways. Who could tell me something that is important to remember when we are practicing +1 facts.

Joe: Never count. It's just one more.

Mrs. Harris: Fantastic, Joe! You remembered. Who wants to give me an example of what Joe is talking about?

Lillian: Like 3 + 1 if 4 . . . you just know . . . like you don't have to count on your fingers . . . you just know it is one more . . .

Mrs. Harris: Yes.

Notice that throughout this conversation, Mrs. Harris is seizing the opportunity to reinforce a very important idea. The students are discussing the idea, and Mrs. Harris is facilitating the conversation. This conversation helps students to concretize their learning in a very student-centered way.

Another part of debriefing the *I can* statements is to have your students talk about where they are on their learning path. Students have to realize that learning is a journey, not just the destination. They should not think, "well, you just learn it." Learning is a path, and different students are in different places. You can use the Marzano (2006) framework, of four levels of understanding as a good framework for structuring the conversation. Your students can rate themselves as doing really well, good, ok, or just starting to learn it (see Chapter 9 for more about this).

Along with this conversation of levels of understanding is a conversation about effort. "Effort meters" are a part of having a growth mindset (Dweck, 2006). The idea is that you should *explicitly* teach students "the harder you try, the more you learn." Instructional structures like effort meters can help your students to reflect on how hard they are really trying (see Figure 8.2).

Figure 8.2 Effort Meter

Today in math class....	
●	I tried really hard. I rocked! The more I try, the more I learn.
●	I tried some. I did not stick with it very long. I need to try harder.
●	I didn't try very hard. I gave up right away. I'll try harder next time.
The more you try, the more you learn!	

Component 2: Shared Thinking/Interactive Class Journal

After your students have had the discussion about the *I can* statements, it is important to give them an opportunity to write about this learning. This should be done in different formats. Sometimes you should have your students do it together with the class as an interactive class math journal, using a big book of chart paper. It should be done in chart paper so that the journals can be kept and referenced in the future. It is important to do interactive thinking journals with your students, because doing this together models what they should do when they have to do it alone (see Figure 8.3).

> **Mr. Thomas:** Ok guys, what are some of your big takeaways from today?
>
> **Tom:** I practiced adding fractions on the computer.
>
> **Susie:** We played a fraction top-it game.
>
> **Timothy:** We worked on solving mixed number story problems with pictures.
>
> **Mr. Thomas:** So, if we wanted to write what we did today, what should we say were some of the most important takeaways?
>
> **Tom:** I would say that you have to remember to make common denominators. Sometimes, I forget to do that.
>
> **Mr. Thomas:** How did the game help you to remember?
>
> **Tom:** It won't let you add them if you do it wrong.
>
> **Mr. Thomas:** What else would we like to add about what we are learning?
>
> **Susie:** When we were playing the Fraction Track game . . . it was hard sometimes. Like when you get 3/4 but you have already moved 3/4, then you have to use other fractions.
>
> **Mr. Thomas:** So what did you learn from that game?
>
> **Susie:** There are many ways to make a fraction. Like we moved 1/2 and 2/8 instead of just the 3/4 marker.
>
> **Mr. Thomas:** How does this help us when working with fractions?
>
> **Marcus:** Well, you can break apart fractions and then add them even in your head. Like if you have 1/2 + 1/8. Then you know 1/2 is 4/8 and 1/8 makes it 5/8.
>
> **Mr. Thomas:** Ok, so let's write some things we're learning.

Figure 8.3 Interactive Thinking

> Today in math class we continued to study fractions. Tom said, "When adding fractions, you have to remember to make common denominators." Susie said, "We also learned that you can make fractions in different ways. You can compose (make) and decompose (break apart) fractions in different ways." Marcus said, "Knowing how to compose and decompose fractions can help you to add quickly in your head."

It is important to do interactive Write Alouds with your students, because this activity gives them a framework for writing in their journals on their own. Having a very specific, intentional conversation about the math that students are doing in their workstations is extremely important, because it helps them to make connections between the activities they are doing in class and the particular content that they are learning. Writing as a whole class is part of the equation. Having your students write on their own is just as important.

Focused Math Writing in the Thinking Journal (aka Math Notebook)

Oftentimes writing exercises in math class are very random. Teachers simply put up prompts like, "What did you learn today?" This is a great start, but you can be more expansive by using focused writing in your math class to summarize the activities for the day. There is a 5-point framework that you can use to get your students to write based on the elements of mathematical proficiency (NRC, 2001). In each unit of study, during the Share, you should use the following prompts:

- Writing for Conceptual Understanding—these are prompts that will get your students to write about the concept they are studying. These prompts also might ask your students to connect the math they are doing to real-life situations.
- Writing for Procedural Fluency—these are prompts that will get your students to write about the procedures they are learning.
- Writing for Strategic Competence—these are prompts that will get your students to use a variety of strategies.
- Writing and Reasoning—these are prompts that will ask your students to either contextualize or decontextualize math problems.
- Writing about Math Disposition—these are prompts that will get your students to write about how they are feeling and doing as learners.

Here is what this exercise might look like:

Second Grade—Unit on Adding Multi-Digit Numbers

Writing for Conceptual Understanding: What does it mean to regroup? Explain using numbers, words, and pictures.

Writing for Procedural Fluency and Strategic Competence: Add 234 and 456. Solve one way and check another.

Reasoning through Writing: Write a story where $234 + 456 = 690$ is the answer.

Writing about Math Disposition: How well do you understand adding three-digit numbers? Well, OK, not yet.

Fourth-Grade Example

Writing for Conceptual Understanding: What does it really mean to multiply $1/2 \times 7$? Explain using numbers, words, and pictures. Another prompt might say, "Give a real-life example of multiplying a whole number by a fraction."

Writing for Procedural Fluency and Strategic Competence: Multiply $3 \times 4/5$. Solve one way and check another.

Reasoning through Writing: Can you tell me a story about $2 \times 3/5$?

Writing about Math Disposition: How well do you understand multiplying a whole number and a fraction? Well, OK, not yet.

During the Share time, you also might ask your students to get together and do a quick group brainstorm of the three most important things about fractions that they have learned this week. After they have brainstormed, the students would either post their charts for everyone to see, or they might share out one or two things that they wrote. Another version of this is to have the students do this activity in their journals and then turn and share with their math partner. Then the students would take turns sharing what each other had learned. This is important (sharing each other's work) because this is part of communicating in math. It requires reading and/or listening to each other's thoughts, thinking about the logic of these thoughts, being able to process this information, and then share it out.

Another way to reflect through writing is to have your students write with exit slips (see more of this in Chapter 10). There are short exit slips and longer ones (see Figures 8.4 and 8.5).

Students can also write reflections about the week.

Figure 8.4 Math Exit Slip

Math Exit Slip
Name:
Date:
2 Things You Learned This Week: (Use numbers, words and pictures) 1. 2. Questions you still have:

Figure 8.5 My Weekly Math Reflections

My Weekly Math Reflections
Name:
Date:
This week I did well with
_____
_____
_____
I need to work on
_____
_____
_____
My plan to get better at _____ is to
_____
_____
_____

There are also electronic exit tickets that you can pull up on various devices, including iPads and laptops (see www.socrative.com/exit-tickets). Sometimes, you can have your students share and write their ticket out the door. There are many ways to frame this. It usually involves some sort of chart or poster on the door (see Figures 8.6, 8.7, 8.8, and 8.9). Various

Figure 8.6 Sample Exit Ticket

What we learned today!
1 2 3 4 5
6 7 8 9 10
11 12 13 14 15
16 17 18 19 20
21 22 23 24 25
26 27 28 29 30
(everybody has a number and they post their response on it)

Figure 8.7 Sample Exit Ticket

Show what you know about multiplication...

(as students leave they put up post-its with examples)

Figure 8.8 Sample Exit Ticket

Show Me the Math!		
Mike said that .09 is more than .1 because 9 is more than 1. Do you agree or disagree with Mike? Answer and explain why.		
I Agree	I'm not sure	I Disagree

headings are used: *What Stuck with You Today?*; *Ticket Out the Door*; *Before You Go—Show What You Know!* There are many different ways to collect this information. Some people put library pockets with numbers on them, and the students slip their tickets into the pocket as they exit the door or as they exit the Share rug. Others have a blank poster that their students paste all over. Others have specific names or numbers, and the students always put theirs in the same place.

Figure 8.9 Sample Exit Ticket

Exit Ticket: Show What You Know about Multiplication

Solve 25 × 14 two different ways.

Way 1	Way 2

How good are you with using different strategies?

Great   Good   Just getting it

Teacher Comments:

Component 3: Share Chair

The Share chair can be a physical place that students sit to share their thinking (commonly done K–3) or just a metaphorical chair (a time) for students to talk to the class about their learning journey. This can be done several ways. Students can share out to the class, to a math partner, or in a group. If this is done in partners or a group, it is important that you time it so everybody gets to share. This is an important part of any Math Workshop, because students need to talk about the concepts and skills they are learning.

Summary

The debriefing is an essential part of Math Workshop. It is a time when your students can make sense of their learning. They make connections between the games they are playing, the activities they are doing, and the videos they are watching, and how these activities are helping them to learn the math. Many times, people skip this section of the Math Workshop because they run out of time. It is crucial that you make time to do this with your students so they can summarize their learning with each other and for themselves.

Key Points

Three components of the Share:

- Recap and discuss the big ideas/*I Can* statements
- Shared thinking/interactive and individual journaling
- The Share chair

Reflection Questions

1. In what ways do you close your math period that helps your students to summarize their learning?
2. What types of writing for learning do you do in your classroom? Do you cover all the different elements of mathematical proficiency?
3. What types of opportunities do you give your students to share their thinking with partners, in a group, and with the whole class?

9

Balanced Assessment

Assessment is the key to a productive Math Workshop. You should have a variety of assessments throughout the year ranging from on-the-spot, in-the-moment, spontaneous assessments, to formal, pre-planned ones. Assessments will help you to know where to begin, how to get there, and what you are doing along the way. Assessments will also tell you if you got there yet. In math instruction, teachers must get much clearer about where their students are, where they want their students to go and how they are going to get the students there. Teachers say things to me like, "Nicki, my students can't add!" I tend to look at them and ask, "What do you mean they can't add? Is it they don't know how to add 0 to a number? Can they not add 1 more to a number? Can they not add through 5? Are they having trouble adding through 10? Do they know their doubles? Is it trouble with doubles plus 1? Or perhaps, doubles plus 2? Or, is it that they can't add 7, 8, or 9 to a number?" And here, I am only questioning about basic facts through 20. My point is that there is a continuum for adding, and it is specific. The more specific you can get with your students, the better you can help them (Newton, 2013).

Slips and Bugs

Ginsberg (1987) theorized that students make two types of mistakes. They either go too quickly and make what he calls "slips"—careless errors that can be easily corrected—or they make "bugs," which are the conceptual or procedural errors. Slips are errors that students can self-correct, while bugs are errors that students need help correcting. For example, when given 200 – 99, many students will write 299 rather than regrouping. This is a procedural and a conceptual error. In a Math Workshop, you would schedule the students who are wrestling with "math bugs" into a guided math group. Two books I highly recommend to learn about helping students with common mathematical errors is *Error Patterns in Computation* (10th ed.) by Ashlock (2009) and *Strategies for Teaching Whole Number Computation* by Spangler (2010).

It is important that you get specific and have a variety of ways to do that. A balanced approach to assessment is an integral part of planning for Math Workshop.

Shepard, Hammerness, Darling-Hammond & Rust (2005) note that formative assessment is framed by three basic questions asked by Atkin, Black, and Coffey (2001, p. 278): (a) Where are you trying to go? (b) Where are you now? and (c) How can you get there?"

Five Strategies for Assessment

Black & Wiliam (2009) identified five strategies that are essential to the successful integration of assessment with instruction:

1. Clarifying and sharing learning intentions and criteria
2. Engineering effective classroom discussions and other learning tasks that elicit evidence of student understanding
3. Providing feedback that moves learners forward
4. Activating students as instructional resources for one another
5. Activating students as the owners of their own learning.

In your classroom, as you think about assessment that improves student achievement, you have to incorporate discussion as an ongoing assessment technique, especially in the opening and closing of each workshop. You have to think about the role of *I can* statements in providing clarity and public learning intentions, criteria, and goals. You have to think about the nature of feedback, so that it is quick, short, and actionable. You have to have your students reflecting on their own learning as well as the learning of others.

Feedback

As Shepard and her colleagues noted, "One of the oldest findings in psychological research (Thorndike, 1931, 1968) is that feedback facilitates learning" (Shepard et al., 2005, p. 287). This type of assessment environment occurs in a culture of collaboration where students believe that the teacher and their fellow students are all in it together, helping each other to learn. Shepard and colleagues stated that:

> This means that feedback must occur strategically throughout the learning process (not at the end when teaching on that topic is finished); teacher and students must have a shared understanding that the purpose of feedback is to facilitate learning; and it may

mean that grading should be suspended during the formative stage. Given that teachers cannot frequently meet one-on-one with each student, classroom practices must allow for students to display their thinking so the teacher will be aware of it, and for students to become increasingly effective critics of their own and each other's work.

(Shepard, et al., 2005, p. 288)

Feedback that is frequent, immediate, and specific can move learning in ways that nothing else can. Students need to learn how to give it and get it, and what to do with it. For example, if a student gets feedback that says the student doesn't know his or her doubles facts, then the student needs to know what to do with that feedback. What's next? How can homework, Math Workstations and guided math groups play a role in addressing that learning goal?

Benchmark Assessments Throughout the Year of Math Workshop

At the beginning of the year, it is crucial to do a formative assessment to see exactly where your students are at that point in their learning. You really are checking to see "what the summer vortex has swallowed!" (Newton, 2013). It is crucial to check the priority standards from the year before. It is important to know what your students have retained. You want to start instruction there. You can't jump into multiplying and dividing fractions if your students have forgotten how to add and subtract fractions—or worse yet, what a fraction is! So, check, check, and check again. Where are they right now? Don't check where they should be, but where they really are. Oftentimes schools will give growth tests. These are fine; they are meant to measure growth. They test the upcoming year's standards at the beginning of the year and then at the end of the year. This is great information to have. However, I still maintain that you have to know if your students know what they are supposed to know, so you can teach your students the new stuff they need to know in the current grade. This Beginning of the Year Benchmark should inform your immediate workstations, your guided math groups, and any whole group review lessons that you do.

The Second Benchmark should be right before the first marking period. This benchmark should cover all of the units covered up until this assessment point. It gives you a great basis for a cumulative grade. It also tells you about retention of knowledge throughout the year. What happened to that September stuff? Is it still there? Will it be there in spring during the state test? How are you ensuring this—with ongoing daily routines and energizers? The Third Benchmark should be right before the second marking period, and it should assess everything that has been taught during that marking period. Finally, towards the end of the year you should give an End of the Year Benchmark to assess what your students have learned that year.

Assessment During the First Part of Math Workshop

The beginning of Math Workshop is a perfect opportunity to assess what your students know. This type of assessment takes place when the entire group is together, talking, and making sense of math as a whole. Individual pupil response systems such as white boards, red/yellow and green cards, and thumbs all serve to let you know where your students are in their learning trajectory. Entrance slips also serve as great indicators of where everybody is. Sometimes entrance slips are anonymous, and other times they have the students' names. They serve as a great thermometer of what is going on and who is getting it, who is completely lost, and who is kinda there! (See Figures 9.1 and 9.2 for examples.)

Figure 9.1 Sample Entrance Ticket

Write everything you know about subtraction in 1 minute. Use numbers, pictures, and words.

Figure 9.2 Sample Entrance Ticket

24 x 59 Show what you know in 2 ways!	
Way 1	Way 2

Ongoing Assessment of Math Centers and Guided Math Groups

It is extremely important to have a system of ongoing assessment in the math centers. This system can be a mix of anecdotes, checklists, artifact sheets, self-assessments, peer assessments, portfolio pieces selected by you and/or your students, quizzes, and general work collected from the work-stations, including fluency quizzes and word problem work. It is important for your students to assess themselves throughout the unit so they can help plan their learning journey. Williams (2011) argues that students should be the "owners of their own learning" as well as "instructional resources" for one another.

Anecdotes
You should take anecdotes throughout Math Workshop. During the whole group lesson, you should make mental notes of who is participating and in what ways. You should also note what happens during the student check-ins (who gets the answer correct and who gets the answer incorrect). At some point in the workshop, be sure to write down these notes so there is a record of them. Some teachers choose students to watch for the day in a very intentional way. Other teachers just take random notes. What is impor-tant is to have a system where you do get to check on everybody.

Checklists
Checklists are also a good way to keep track of student learning. They are especially great because they allow you to assess your students, students to assess themselves, and students to assess other students. See Figure 9.3 for an example of a fifth-grade math standard broken down in a way so as to provide an exact excavation of the standard. Students should have to provide evidence that they can actually do the things. This evidence comes through workstation activities, homework, quizzes, and self-assessments.

Math Workstation Artifact Sheets

Your students should keep artifact sheets from the workstations that they visit. By keeping these in a folder with red and green dots, then it is clear what they are working on and what they have finished. Figure 9.4 is an example of a math artifact sheet. In this sheet, the students are working on a fraction unit. When they go to the workstation, they use a double dice to generate the fraction. Then they have to write the fraction and the fraction word, and plot the fraction on a number line.

Self-Assessments

Self-assessments are very important. Your students need to continually think about what they know, what they don't know, and how they are

Figure 9.3 Standard Broken Down as a Checklist

Fifth-Grade Fraction Standard			
Find whole-number quotients of whole numbers with up to four-digit dividends and two-digit divisors using strategies based on place value, the properties of operations and/or the relationship between multiplication and division. Illustrate and explain the calculation by using equations, rectangular arrays and/or area models.			
I can divide in many different ways.	Yes	No	Somewhat
I can find whole-number quotients of whole numbers with one-digit dividends and one-digit divisors.	Yes	No	Somewhat
I can find whole-number quotients of whole numbers with two-digit dividends and one-digit divisors.	Yes	No	Somewhat
I can find whole-number quotients of whole numbers with three-digit dividends and one-digit divisors.	Yes	No	Somewhat
I can find whole-number quotients of whole numbers with three-digit dividends and one-digit divisors.	Yes	No	Somewhat
I can find whole-number quotients of whole numbers with four-digit dividends and one-digit divisors.	Yes	No	Somewhat
I can find whole-number quotients of whole numbers with two-digit dividends and two-digit divisors.	Yes	No	Somewhat
I can find whole-number quotients of whole numbers with three-digit dividends and two-digit divisors.	Yes	No	Somewhat
I can find whole-number quotients of whole numbers with four-digit dividends and two-digit divisors.	Yes	No	Somewhat
I can use strategies based in place value to divide.	Yes	No	Somewhat
I can use properties to divide.	Yes	No	Somewhat
I can use the relationship between multiplication and division to divide.	Yes	No	Somewhat
I can illustrate and explain the calculation by using equations.	Yes	No	Somewhat
I can illustrate and explain the calculation by using rectangular arrays.	Yes	No	Somewhat
I can illustrate and explain the calculation by using the area models.	Yes	No	Somewhat

going to learn it, in conjunction with you. Self-assessments hold your students accountable for their learning trajectory. Your students should also have individual student response systems so that during different times during the workshop (whether in a whole group setting, workstations, or in the guided math group), they can indicate their level of learning (see Figure 9.5).

Figure 9.4 Math Artifact Sheet

Name:

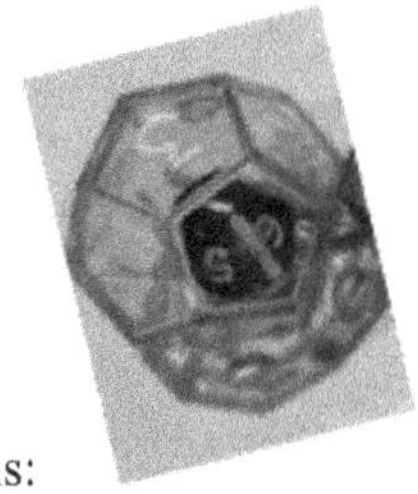

Game Instructions:

Roll the double dice.
Inside Number = denominator
Outside Number = numerator

    1. Fraction: _____
    2. Fraction Word _____
    3. Plot the fraction on the number line
    4. Compare the fraction to a number that is greater than this fraction
       using <, >, =.

Figure 9.5 Self-Assessment

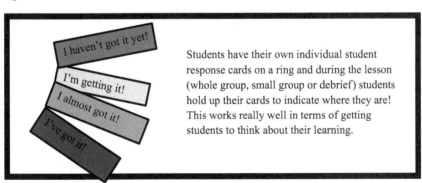

I haven't got it yet!

I'm getting it!

I almost got it!

I've got it!

Students have their own individual student response cards on a ring and during the lesson (whole group, small group or debrief) students hold up their cards to indicate where they are! This works really well in terms of getting students to think about their learning.

Tracking Self-Assessments through *I Can* Statement Charts

Marzano (2006) talks about the four different levels of understanding. In Marzano's framework there is also a level 0, a level before level 1. He says that you can use this rating scale before instruction, during instruction, and after instruction.

Figure 9.6 Quick Check Ratings

Quick Check	Quick Check
How are you doing with fractions?	Got It! Almost! Getting it! Not Yet!
What are you doing well with?	
What do you still need help with?	
What are you going to do?	
What can Ms. Lee do to help?	

Figure 9.7 Self-Assessment Linked to *I Can* Statements

0	1	2	3	4
I don't get any of it yet!	I can do it with a lot of help!	I can do some of it with help.	I can do it by myself.	I know it so well that I can teach somebody else how to do it.
Explain your thinking with numbers, words, and pictures.				

Self-assessments are linked to the *I can* statements. A self-assessment can be done in a variety of ways, starting at a young age. For example, in the first grade, the goal is to be able to add and subtract within 10. The *I can* statements might be:

I can add +0 facts.
I can add +1 facts.
I can add +2 facts.
I can add +3 facts.
I can add any facts within 5.
I can add facts within 10.

One way to help your students keep track of their work is to have crayons with these goals written on them. As your students progress through these facts, they get to color the crayons, teddy bears, or whatever symbol on their goal page. The students stay motivated and know exactly what they are moving towards. Self-assessments also can involve students writing about how much they have learned and what they still need to know. See a sample goal page in Figure 9.8.

Figure 9.8 Sample Goal Page

I can count to 100!

Self-Assessment of Chapter Tests

It is also very important for your students to always reflect on chapter tests (see Figures 9.6 and 9.7). They should note what they did really well on, what they missed and how they are going to study to learn the things they are still struggling with. Figure 9.9 shows an example of a student post-test reflection. Figure 9.10 shows a teacher's reflection on the test.

Figure 9.9 Post-Test Reflection

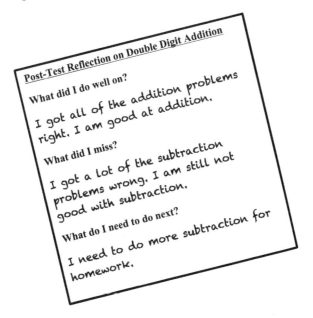

Post-Test Reflection on Double Digit Addition

What did I do well on?

I got all of the addition problems right. I am good at addition.

What did I miss?

I got a lot of the subtraction problems wrong. I am still not good with subtraction.

What do I need to do next?

I need to do more subtraction for homework.

Figure 9.10 Post-Test Reflection

<u>Teacher Notes on Double Digit Addition</u>

What did you do well on?

Jamal you got all of the addition problems correct! Good going!

What did you miss?

You missed 3 out of the 5 subtraction problems.

What do you need to do next?

We need to meet in a guided math group about subtraction. I also will give you some homework problems.

I want you to spend some extra time working with subtraction in the math workstations. You can play subtraction games on the computer! You will get there! Keep trying!

Self-Assessment in Journals

Journals are a great, permanent record of students' self-reflections. There are several prompts that you can ask students to use to unpack their thinking about their progress. Sometimes, you should give a direct prompt, but other times you should give a list to choose from. Figure 9.11 shows some examples of journal prompts.

Figure 9.12 is another example of a chart that can give your students a framework for talking about their learning journey.

Peer Assessments

It is also important to have your students look at each other's work and be able to discuss it intelligently. In order to look at each other's work and give meaningful feedback, students need to practice giving it and receiving it. Use protocols, because then your students have a checklist, and the feedback and conversation is guided by the checklist (see Figure 9.13 for a primary grade protocol).

Teachers have to set aside time to teach students how to evaluate each other's work. This is so worth it, because in learning to evaluate the work

Figure 9.11 Sample Journal Prompts

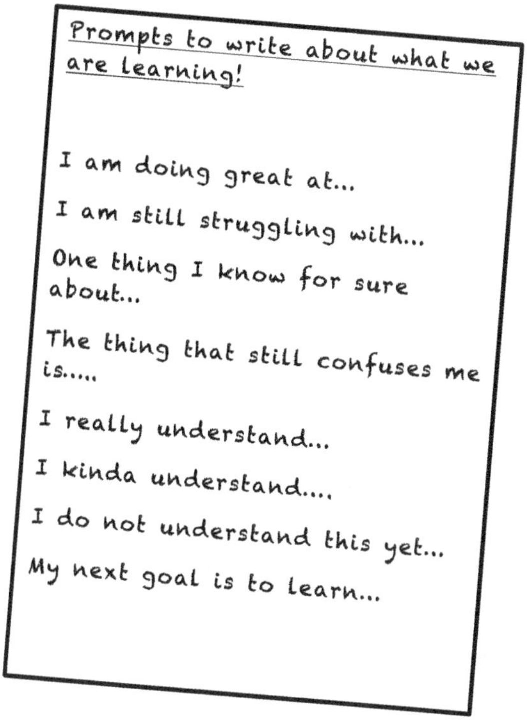

<u>Prompts to write about what we
are learning!</u>

I am doing great at...

I am still struggling with...

One thing I know for sure
about...

The thing that still confuses me
is.....

I really understand...

I kinda understand....

I do not understand this yet...

My next goal is to learn...

Figure 9.12 Chart for Talking About Learning

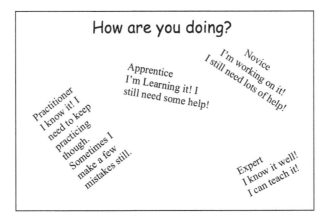

of others, students learn how to improve their own work. Students need to know how to give each other feedback in helpful rather than hurtful ways. I find that checklists help students to stay on track because they are working from a scaffolded template (see Figure 9.14 for an upper elementary example of a peer assessment rubric).

Figure 9.13 Peer Word Problem Checklist

Peer Word Problem Checklist			
	Yes	No	Somewhat
Is there a model? Drawing Number line Ten frame Other:			
Is there a set-up equation with a symbol for the missing part?			
Is the answer correct?			
Comments			

Figure 9.14 Peer Assessment Rubric

Peer Assessment Rubric		
Original Mathematician: Name of checker		
	Yes	No
Did the mathematician solve the problem?		
Did the mathematician model his or her thinking?		
Did the mathematician write an equation?		
Did the mathematician use math words?		
Did the mathematician check the answer in a different way than he or she did at first?		
Did the mathematician explain his or her thinking with words?		
Comments:		

Class Assessments

There are many different ways to check in with students. Taking a *Status of the Class* is a way to help your students to self-monitor their progress with the *I can* statements in a unit of study. These ideas reflect Marzano's theory of the four levels of understanding (Marzano, 2006) and aligning them with data. There are many ways to do this. Your students could write their name on a sticky note and place it where they are in the learning continuum. Or, each student could be assigned a number (that only you and the student know about) and each student posts a sticky note with his or her number on the chart. Either way, this is a way for students to self-reflect.[1]

Brandi (2012) expanded on Marzano's (2006) idea of students tracking their data and used it as a way to discuss data from tests with students. I would use it a little differently. I would have the students self-reflect on how they see themselves learning the new content. I would have them place themselves in the appropriate category, and then on free-choice workstation days, have them make choices based on what they want/need to get better at doing. This is also a great way to end the workshop by discussing the *Status of the Class*.

Portfolio Pieces Selected by the Teacher and/or the Student

It is really important for your students to get to choose work they are proud of and explain why the work proves that they know the standards for the grade level. There are a growing number of sites that even allow this work to be stored on the Internet, free of charge for teachers, in portfolios. Some portals even allow for both teachers and students to post the work with explanations, videos, and podcasts.

Quizzes

It is important to give formal quizzes at least twice during a unit of study to make sure that your students are progressing successfully through the unit goals. If you give quizzes in the middle of a unit, then you and your students have time to course correct, rather than waiting until the end of the unit and resulting in a bunch of students who did not learn what they needed to in the unit. The quizzes should be short, to the point, and rigorous. By that, I mean that they should consist of multiple choice, short answer, and extended response questions. They should also have not only Depth of Knowledge (DOK) level 1 questions, but also DOK level 2 and 3 questions. Figure 9.15 shows an example.

Fluency Quizzes

Fluency is an essential component of elementary mathematics. Each grade level has a designated fluency. You should have ongoing quizzes around fluency; however, they should never terrorize your students. You want your students to know their facts fluently. Fluency means not only automaticity, but also flexibility and efficiency. I am a big advocate of having Fun Fact Fluency folders (a name made popular by some teachers in Arkansas that I work with) so that students can begin to see their practice as engaging.

Figure 9.15 Odd and Even Quiz

Odd and Even Quiz
Name
Date

I can determine whether a group of objects (up to 20) has an odd or even number of members. I can pair them or count by 2's.

1. Look at the puffins. Are there an even or odd number of them? How do you know?

Explain your answer below.

2. Circle all the odd numbers below.

3   5   6   8

9   10   11

23   56   90

3. Draw an even number of marbles. Explain why it is an even number.

4. Write a doubles fact. Explain why the sum is even using numbers, words and pictures.

One way to do this is to have folders where students are working towards their grade-level fluency, and they take quizzes at their own pace. They evaluate their quizzes and then, along with you, they decide on the next steps. Figure 9.16 shows an example of a quiz. This quiz can be taken with time. The students know they should be able to pass it quickly, somewhere between 40 and 60 seconds. The research generally says three seconds per problem, so technically this quiz should be done in 33 seconds. I always tell the students we are just going for quick, and so they should try to keep working until they get somewhere in the stated range.

Figure 9.16 Fluency Quiz

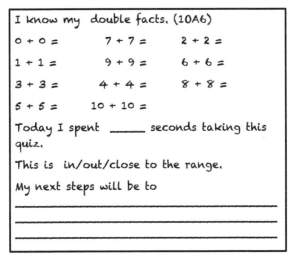

Newton 2013

Word Problem Work

In the word problem workstation, you should have ongoing assessments to see what levels of problems your students are working on. The assessments should vary. In every unit of study, there should be problem solving. The problem assessments should vary. Figures 9.17, 9.18, and 9.19 show a few examples of what the assessments might look like. As you will notice, different assessments give different types of information. The assessment

Figure 9.17 Assessment of Whether Students Can Contextualize a Word Problem

Twenty marbles is the answer; what is the question?

Figure 9.18 Assessment of Whether Students Can Recognize a Type of Problem

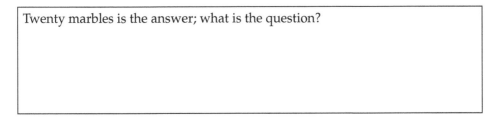

Figure 9.19 Assessment for Problem Solving Practice

Sue had 50 centimeters of string. She went to the store and bought 40 more centimeters to make jewelry. How much string does she have altogether now?	Solve the problem using a model. Write an equation: _____ Answer: _____
Check your answer a different way than you first solved it.	Explain what you did to find the answer.

in Figure 9.17 tells whether or not students can contextualize a word problem, which is a part of mathematical reasoning. The assessment in Figure 9.18 tells whether or not students can recognize the type of problem they are solving so they know what to do. Many students who have problems with problem solving do not know what type of operation to use to solve the problems. The assessment in Figure 9.19 looks at problem solving.

Vocabulary Work

Math is a language, and if you expect your students to learn it, then you have to get them to speak it! Teachers also have to speak it to them! Children need vocabulary to express their thoughts. They need vocabulary to comment on each other's thoughts as well. "In content area reading, students need a thorough understanding of vocabulary because the words are labels for important concepts" (Harmon, Hedrick & Wood, 2005, p. 265).

In the vocabulary center, students should do a variety of work that shows they know the vocabulary and they know how to distinguish from everyday words and math words. Some researchers have pointed out that "Many terms have meanings in the realm of mathematics that differ from their meanings in everyday usage" (Monroe & Orme, 2002, p. 140). For example, students hear: "The ball is round. The table is round. The sphere is round." You have to explicitly show how some math words sound like other words, such as Sum and Some. You also must talk about how some math words have different meanings in math than in everyday life, like Table and Chair versus "Put those numbers in a table" (see Figure 9.20).

Figure 9.20 Assessment for Evidence of Vocabulary Mastery

Decimal Vocabulary Quiz

1. Describe what **tenths** means below.

2. Circle the **thousandths** in the number below.
   2.4568

3. Write the word form of this number: .02

Face-to-Face Assessments

It is important to talk with your students about their learning. You can find out a variety of different types of things when you question your students. There are some students who are not great test takers, but they can explain exactly what they know verbally. Students should be required to be able to express themselves in all ways. Explaining their thinking out loud should be a daily routine, whether they are turning and talking with a partner, sharing ideas in a group, or talking with you in a math interview or one-to-one conference.

Interviews

Part of a balanced assessment system includes talking with your students face to face and finding out what they know by listening to them. Math interviews and math conferences are an important part of finding out what your students do and do not know. A math interview is different from a conference. A math interview is more like a verbal quiz. It is quantitative. You give the student a set of tasks and/or problems to work on. These are preplanned. However, during the interview you might have a series of tasks going from simple to more complex. Math interviews can give so much information in just a few questions. For example, you might ask a student a series of questions about what is 8 + 7. You can find out if the student can think strategically about the problem, has automaticity, and can model the fact. You also gain insight into the student's mathematical disposition (how the student thinks and feels about himself or herself as a learner of mathematics). See Figure 9.21 for an example of a math interview.

Figure 9.21 Math Interview

What is the answer to 8 + 7?	What are some different strategies for thinking about 8 + 7?
Can you model 8 + 7?	Do you think this is an easy fact to remember or a hard fact to remember?

During the interview, you will ask the questions, but there should be plenty of opportunity for the student to talk and explain his or her thinking and actions. Many math interviews have a performance aspect to them, oftentimes using manipulatives (even in the upper elementary grades). The teacher prompts the students with questions such as " Can you . . .? How do you . . .? Show me how to . . . ." Remember that in an interview, you should maintain neutrality towards the task. If the student asks for help, you should throw the question back at the student by asking things like, "what do you think?" or "do you think you're right?" (www.txar.org/ assessment/flex/MTCK2_FlexInterviewGuidelines.pdf).

Conferences

Math conferences are about talking with the students and finding out something specific about their procedures, conceptual understanding, reasoning, disposition, or strategic competence. During conferences, there is a much more back-and-forth exchange and there is a goal-setting period. Some days you will confer with the students and take notes on those conferences. Figure 9.22 is an example of notes that a teacher might take during a math conference. In this example, the teacher simply circles the type of

Figure 9.22 Math Conferences

Math Conference:

Conceptual Procedural **Strategic Competence** Adaptive Reasoning Disposition

Today talked with Luke about different strategies for division. I asked him which 2 strategies he could do. He did traditional method and open array. He explained that open array was easy when you started with hundreds, then went to tens, then ones.

Here is what he did:

PASTE PICTURE OF STICKY NOTE HERE

Next Steps: Pull Luke into a guided math group and work on illustrating and explaining division using the area model.

conference, records what happens, and attaches an artifact from the conference. This can be done easily if the students do the work on sticky notes.

Assessments During the Debriefing

Discussion
During the debriefing, there are many opportunities for assessment. You can lead a discussion that reveals what your students do and do not understand. Sometimes it is a good idea to put up a chart and then discuss where everyone is along the journey. One way to do this is to have the students put stickers up under labels of how they evaluate themselves. Along with this chart is a recap of what they are supposed to know, and more importantly, what each person feels he or she needs to do in terms of next steps. Figure 9.23 shows an example of a chart that can be used for discussion during a debriefing.

Figure 9.23 Chart for Discussion During Debriefing

How much we know about multiplication so far.....		
We know a great deal	We know some...we need to learn some more	We are still learning....we only know a little so far

Exit Slips
Another assessment strategy you can use during the debriefing is to have your students fill out exit slips reflecting on their learning that day. Just as with entrance slips, exit slips check for procedures, conceptual understanding, reasoning, strategic competence, and disposition. Figure 9.24 shows examples of exit slips.

Traditional Assessments

Homework and chapter tests are linchpins of classroom assessment. I think it is important to rethink these traditional assessments. In terms of homework, I think it is much more valuable to give one problem and have the students do several things with it than to give 10 problems and have the students do one thing with it. Figure 9.25 is an example of a weekly homework assignment.

Figure 9.24 Exit Slips

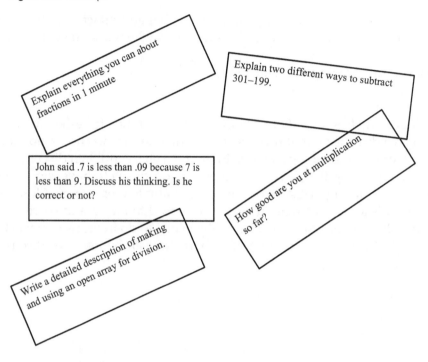

Explain everything you can about fractions in 1 minute

Explain two different ways to subtract 301–199.

John said .7 is less than .09 because 7 is less than 9. Discuss his thinking. Is he correct or not?

How good are you at multiplication so far?

Write a detailed description of making and using an open array for division.

Figure 9.25 Sample Homework Assignment

Homework: Working with two-digit numbers

I can multiply two-digit numbers in more than one way.

I can model my thinking using an open array, an area model, and equations.

Part A. Solve these problems:

	Solve Traditional Way	Solve Another Way
12 x 15		
15 x 17		
19 x 22		

Part B: Explain how knowing different strategies helps you to be a more flexible and efficient mathematician.

In terms of the chapter test, you must expose your students to DOK level 1, level 2, and level 3 problems. The assessments should mirror the types of questions that your students will be asked on statewide assessments, if your students are going to be prepared for the test. Although teachers should not teach to the test, teachers are held accountable for whether or not their students can pass the test. So, your cumulative chapter assessments should mirror the rigor that your students will see on the high-stakes test. There should be multiple-choice, short-answer, extended response as well as vocabulary questions.

Summary

Assessment drives the Math Workshop. At the beginning of the workshop, you can check in with your students. During the student activity period, there are several opportunities for students to show their learning, and then again at the end of the workshop, students have another opportunity to assess their learning. There should be a good mix of teacher assessment, student assessment, and peer assessment. There should be a variety of assessments to get a fuller picture of student learning. Students should receive feedback that they can act on. After the assessment, each student should know what to work on and how to work on it. As Wiggins & McTighe (2005, p. 152) noted, "assessment should be a scrapbook rather than a snapshot" (see Figure 9.26).

Benchmarks at key moments throughout the year and pre-assessments at the beginning of each chapter serve to avoid frustration and/or absolute redundancy/boredom. Ongoing assessment allows you multiple ways to monitor progress of the work done. When you monitor throughout the unit, you can catch students who are failing to understand rather than waiting to find that out at the end of the unit. It is crucial to have assessments and self-reflections at the end of the chapter that allow your students to self-evaluate and consider their scores, where they are, and where they need to go so they can make a plan to get there.

Key Points

- It is important to have a variety of assessments
- Remember that students either make slips or bugs (Ginsberg, 1987)
- Assessment should be done throughout the math workshop
- During the introduction, students can have a discussion or fill out entrance slips
- You should constantly be assessing the work done in math workstations and guided math groups

Figure 9.26 Chart of Components of Balanced Assessment in Math Workshop

Components of Balanced Assessment in Math Workshop			
Type	Specific Assessments	Explanation	When
Benchmark Assessments (landmark exams given throughout the year to assess student learning)	Beginning of the Year Benchmark	Major cluster tests from year before; vocabulary tests; mathematical disposition; math fluency from prior grade level	First Month of School
	1st Cumulative Assessment of Current Grade's Standards	Assessing all taught topics	1st Grading Period
	2nd Cumulative Assessment of Current Grade's Standards	Assessing all taught topics	2nd Grading Period
	End of the Year Benchmark	On grade-level assessments – Major cluster, vocabulary, mathematical disposition; fluency	Last Month of the School Year
Math Workshop Opening	Discussion	An opening discussion about the day's, week's, or unit's learning (makes connections to the essential questions of the unit and/or the *I can* statements)	Daily
	Entrance Slips	A check-in at the beginning of the lesson that is written about something in the unit assessing a component of mathematical proficiency	At least two or three times during the unit
	Individual Pupil Response Systems	Opportunities for students to answer using various response systems	Daily

Math Workstations/ Guided Math		Description	Frequency
	Anecdotes/ Observations	Teacher observations and notes about student learning	Often
	Checklists	A quick itemized list of student goals	At least two times during the unit
	Artifact Sheets	Collection of the work that students do in Math Workstations or guided math groups	Collect weekly
	Self-Assessments	An assessment of the student of their own work	Collect weekly
	Peer Assessment	An assessment by a student peer	At least two or three times during a unit
	Portfolio	A collection of student work chosen by the student and/or teacher	At least once or twice during a unit
	Vocabulary	Different types of assessments to determine if students know the vocabulary associated with the unit of study	Four to six different activities with vocabulary per unit of study (bingo, charades, flash cards, tic-tac-toe, etc.)
Debriefing	Discussion	A wrap-up discussion about the day's, week's, or unit's learning (ties back to the essential questions of the unit and/or the *I can* statements)	Daily
	Exit Slips	A check-in at the end of the lesson that is written about something in the unit assessing a component of mathematical proficiency	Often
Face-to-Face Assessments	Math Interviews	Verbal assessment of student learning	At least one time during a unit and/or grading period
	Math Conferences	A one-to-one discussion that checks the elements of mathematical proficiency	At least one time during a unit and/or grading period
Traditional Assessments	Homework	Practice problems	Daily or weekly
	Chapter Test	End of unit summative assessment	End of the unit

- Be sure to do some face-to-face assessments; they will reveal things that you can never find out with paper-and-pencil exams
- During the debriefing, again do check-ins through discussion and exit slips
- Self-assessments are a vital part of the workshop, and they should be done throughout the math workshop and then after the chapter test
- Peer assessments help students to learn more about the topic by monitoring the work of others based on the criteria that they too must use

Reflection Questions

1. Do you feel like you have a balanced math assessment approach? Do you give your students several opportunities to show evidence of learning throughout the unit?
2. Do you have all three types of assessment opportunities: teacher assessments, self-assessments, and peer assessments?
3. How often do you self-reflect throughout the chapter? How do you know that what you are collecting is worthwhile? How does what you assess inform what you do next?
4. What are three ideas that you can implement right away or in a different way from this chapter? Why did you choose those three?

Note

1. Idea from Brandi (http://myteacherfriend.blogspot.com/2012/10/math-benchmark-tracking.html) and Sarah K. (http://misskinbk.blogspot.com/2013/03/using-data-to-drive-choices-in-math.html).

10

Action Planning
A Quick-Start Guide

Start today. Start small. Be confident. Do it step by step.
Dr. Nicki Newton

1. *Question: How do I get started?*
   Make a plan. Think about how long your math block is. What is the time frame you have to work with? What is the math program you have to work with? What are your big goals for the unit and the year? Do your students know about them? Is everybody on board? Decide on the elements of the workshop. Oftentimes people will start with just one or two elements of the workshop. For example, you might just start by trying to do some interesting mini-lessons and then still do your whole-group lessons. You might start by trying out workstations one or two days a week. It is always better to start slow and be prompted forward by success than to jump in and drown! So go slow.

2. *Question: How do I do this along with our designated math curriculum?*
   Math Workshop is an instructional framework for your math block. You can incorporate your program into the structure. There are many different ways to do it. Sometimes, teachers will teach their regular program two or three times a week, and do Math Workshop stations and guided math groups the other times. Sometimes, teachers will do the program lesson as their mini-lesson and then pull guided math groups while the other students work in stations. Teachers also look at the elements of a lesson and decide which parts could be put into workstations for ongoing practice.

3. *Question: How do I start workstations? Like, literally what is the first thing I should do?*
   At the beginning of the year, always consider the priority standards from last year. This is a great starting point, because it is content that

students should know, and yet many still need ongoing practice with these standards. Also, start playing games with your class as a whole class, in teams, and in small groups so that your students can learn some game structures that can be an ongoing part of workstations. For example, the Power Tower game is a great game structure to teach your students, because then they can do it across different math topics. Another example is making different types of interactive books. Once your students learn to make a flip book they can make it to show understanding across various topics like money, measurement, and geometry.

Next, remember that less is more. Do not try to have a different game every day or even every week. Workstations are about purposeful practice. So, take the time to set up some great dice, domino, and card activities, and then use those to work on many topics. Use game activity sheets so the students can use them over and over again. Always think in terms of developmentally appropriate activities. Remember that students will practice math facts ten times more on purple popsicle sticks than they will on a boring worksheet!

Take the time to practice the workstations and also to have your students practice moving in and out of them. This is the glue of the workshop. Transitions are important. They can make or break the workshop. Your students should work at this routine and perfect it before you start doing workstations and guided math groups together. Decide if you are going to have your students move or if you are going to make the workstations portable. Either way works, but I do think portable workstations can save time.

Have task cards. Task cards remind students of what they are supposed to be doing. Each task card should have the name of the game, the *I can* statement, and the instructions to the game. Task cards can be handwritten or typed. The recording sheets can also go right in the envelope with each task card.

4. *Question: How do I hold the students accountable to workstation work?*
One way to start is to have an accountability sheet at every workstation. Eventually, once you feel that your students truly understand the process and are working well, you can move to some games that don't require writing down everything. There are so many activity recording sheets on the web, so this is an easy way to start.

Also, it is important to have some time to go and visit the workstations every week. This gives you an opportunity to pop into groups, do group interviews, do observations, take anecdotes, and sit and work with groups. You can get a feel for not only the individual work, but also the partner and group dynamics.

You will get to see and evaluate the teamwork and the task work. It is highly recommended that you also have some sort of reward system in place for groups that always work well together. Your students should be rewarded for working well and getting things done. This could be a verbal praise or some other sort of reward system. Also, have your students talk about their work together. What are they learning from each other? How are they helping each other? What do they do when somebody gets stuck? Take the time to find these things out on your free days.

5. *Question: What about the pacing guide and the text?*
The pacing guide can be great. It helps us move along, so that we don't spend half of the year in one chapter. However, the pacing guide sometimes feels like a Mack Truck backing us up against a brick wall. Pacing guides can give us a landscape view. We can see where we have to go. Math Workstations and guided math groups give teachers an "in the trenches view." They tell us exactly where we are and allow us to do "the work" then and there. So, we have to look at the pacing guide and realize that we can keep talking about the big ideas, but that everybody might not get them in three days. The pacing guide and the text might allow only three days to teach doubles or how to multiply a fraction, whereas we know our students need more days than this. Therefore, use the guided math groups to pull them and teach them what they need to know, to fill in gaps, teach concepts from a conceptual, then pictorial and finally abstract perspective. Allow your students to practice in their zone of proximal development in the workstations.

Differentiate—meaning, teach your students what they need to know to know what they need to know. Stop, and read that again. Yes, teach your students what they need to know in order to learn what they need to know. Guided math groups and Math Workstations allow you to do just this. The text is great for students who are on grade level. What about everybody else? Some folks need to go ahead and others need to go back and pick up some things first.

The text. . . . Why is it in math we say everybody on the same page at the same time? In literacy, more often than not, we teach students in their zone of proximal development. We never say, "Today everybody is going to read M books. It doesn't matter if you are a Z reader or an A reader, today everyone is an M reader." But we do this silliness in math. We say, "We are studying doubles +1 facts." It often seems irrelevant that some students can't even make five or ten or know their doubles. But it should be and it is. So let's think and ponder how we can actually get everyone to learn their doubles +1 facts by the end of the year. Although many bought curriculums are helpful, we have to decide if we are teaching the text or the students.

Debbie Miller, author of *Reading with Meaning*, said, "We cannot choose fidelity to a program, curriculum, or test over fidelity to a child" (Miller, http://catchingreaders.com/quotes/). We have to make some mathematically sound decisions if we really want to see students move towards mathematical proficiency.

6. *Question: What about the Chapter Assessments?*
We have to think about what information the assessments give us. Where is there room for the growing mathematician? I think chapter quizzes and assessments give us information about the ongoing progress. Curriculum-based assessments allow us to do quarterly check-ins to see how it is going as well. We should do more interviews and grade-created assessments. The assessments should be scaffolded so we can see exactly how our students are progressing. There should be a way to show progress towards the goal. This requires a paradigm shift, because this isn't the way we teach in math right now. However, some schools do require students to have an intervention plan if students score below a certain percentage, and then they have to retake the test. The question always then becomes: Is it a merger of the two scores, or do they get the highest score? If we are teaching so that students learn, then they should get credit for learning!

7. *Question: What do I do with the children who cannot work independently?*
Everybody can work independently doing something. Have your students practice something that they **do** know how to do, even if it is prerequisite knowledge from the year before or from earlier in the year. Scaffold the activity as much as possible and teach them how to do it. For example, with kindergarten and first grade, I would put a geometry center out—one that includes play dough and puzzles so that students can play around with shapes. I would also set up some number writing centers, with sand, gel, and crayons. In second- and third-grade classrooms, I would set up addition and multiplication centers where students can actually build the facts. In fourth- and fifth-grade classrooms, I would put up multiplication and fraction centers. Students always need to review basic facts and oftentimes work with manipulatives to do this.

8. *Question: How do I manage the toolkits?*
Yes, you need toolkits. Yes, they can be quite messy and unorganized in the beginning. Yes, your students really do need them. They are an immense help. They scaffold thinking in so many ways. They allow for growing independence. There are many ways to do this. Ideally, every student has his or her own kit. At first this can seem daunting. However, it doesn't have to be. Introduce the tools a few at a time.

Only after the students have practiced using the tools should they go into the toolkits. In the beginning, you can also review tools from prior years that your students will be using this year in a different way. For example, the teddy bears that everybody thinks are only for kindergarten are really for every grade. You can teach basic number facts, comparison, addition and subtraction, multiplication and division, and fraction and ratios with these manipulatives. Don't underestimate the power of the bear! Or any of those other manipulatives that seem like primary ones but should actually be used in the upper elementary grades as well (i.e., Unifix cubes and two-sided counters).

In terms of logistics, there are a couple of ways to store toolkits. One way is to have each student be individually responsible for his or her own toolkit. Another way is to have a community tool chest with the toolkits inside them. Any time someone needs a tool kit, he or she can just grab one. Still a third way is to have table kits that are shared in a group. There is no one correct way to do this. You know your students. Every class is different. I like individual toolkits because they are there at the ready, so when a student needs it, the student can use it quickly. Make sure to spend time on the cleanup routine, so your students know not only how to clean up and put back the toolkits, but that they also know how to make sure that the toolkits are put back intact. One idea is to make a big tool checklist so your students can make sure everything is back in the kit before they put it away.

9. *Question: How do I know how it is going?*
It is imperative that we reflect on our process. That's how we get better. That's how we go from good to great. How are you evaluating your Math Workshop? What structures do you have in place? Think about what is going really well. Congratulate yourself. Now, how can you bump it up just a notch? What is going ok? Just name one thing you can do to improve it. Now, what is not working? How do you rethink what is not going well? It is ok to stop doing something. It's ok to "have a go" and then say, "no, this doesn't work for me and my students." Or, "yes this could work, but I have to change it this way or that way." Own the process. Own making the mistakes. Then, own the success!

10. *Question: How do we go from good to great with Math Workshop in our school?*
Work together. Make time to visit each other's classrooms to see how different people are doing it. Go in with an eye to catch your colleagues being good. What is it that they do really well that you could incorporate into your workshop? Do grade visitations and peer visitations where you go in with a specific protocol to look and learn something new. Have people talk about their expertise and something they could use help with.

Figure 10.1 Going from Good to Great: Math Workstation Intervisitation

Going from Good to Great: Math Workstation Intervisitation	
1. Team Members:	2. Today we are looking at: *Opening:* • *Energizers/Routines* • *Number Talk* • *Mini-Lesson* *Student Activity* • *Workstations* • *Guided Math Group* • *Conferring/Interviews* • *Seminar* *Debrief* • *I can reflection* • *Journaling* • *Mathematicians Chair*
3. We saw . . . 4. We heard . . .	5. We wondered . . .

References

Allsopp, D.H., Kyger, M.M., & Lovin, L.H. (2007). *Teaching mathematics meaningfully: Solutions for reaching struggling learners.* Baltimore, MD: Paul H. Brooks.

Armstrong, T. (2009). *Multiple intelligences in the classroom* (3rd ed.). Alexandria, VA: ASCD.

Ashlock, R.B. (2006). *Error patterns in computation: Using error patterns to help each student learn* (3rd ed.). Boston, MA: Allyn and Bacon.

Atkin, J.M., Black, P., & Coffey, J. (2001). *Classroom assessment and the national science standards.* Washington, DC: National Academies Press.

Bafile, C. (2001). *Math and literature: A match made in the classroom.* www.educationworld.com/a_curr/curr249.shtml

Black, P., & Wiliam, D. (2009). Developing the theory of formative assessment. *Educational Assessment, Evaluation and Accountability, 21,* 5–31.

Chapin, S.H., O'Connor, C., & Anderson, N.C. (2003). *Classroom discussions: Using math talk to help students learn.* Sausalito, CA: Math Solutions.

Cirillo, M. (2013). *What are some strategies for facilitating productive classroom discussions?* NCTM Research Brief. S. DeLeeuw, Series Editor. Reston, VA: National Council of Teachers of Mathematics. www.nctm.org/news/content.aspx?id=35386

Clements, D., & Sarama, J. (2009). *Learning and teaching early math. The learning trajectories approach.* New York: Routledge.

Diller, D. (2003). *Literacy workstations: Making centers work.* Portland, ME: Stenhouse.

Dweck, C. (2006). *Mindset, the new psychology of success.* New York: Random House.

Fosnot, C., & Uttenbogaard, W. (2008). *Minilessons for early addition and subtraction.* Portsmouth, NH: Heinemann.

Fountas, I., & Pinnell, G.S. (1996). *Guided reading.* Portsmouth, NH: Heinemann.

Ginsburg, H.P. (1987). The development of arithmetic thinking. In D.D. Hammill (Ed.), *Assessing the abilities and instructional needs of students* (pp. 423–440). Austin, TX: PRO-ED.

Goos, M. (2004). Learning mathematics in a classroom community of inquiry. *Journal for Research in Mathematics Education, 35*(4), 258–291.

Harmon, J., Hedrick, W., & Wood, K. (2005). Research on vocabulary instruction in the content areas: Implication for struggling readers. *Reading & Writing Quarterly, 21,* 261–280.

Hattie, J. (2009). *Visible learning: A synthesis of 800 meta-analyses relating to achievement*. New York: Routledge.

Hunter, R., & Anthony, G. (2011). Teaching and learning research initiative. Learning to "friendly argue" in a community of mathematical inquiry. http://foxwellforest.blogspot.com/p/about-me.html

Illustrative Mathematics. (2014). Standards for mathematical practice: Commentary and elaborations for K–5. Tucson, AZ.

Jobe, R., & Dayton-Sakari, M. (1999). *Reluctant readers*. York, ME: Pembroke.

Johnson, D.W., Johnson, R., & Smith, K. (1998). *Active learning: Cooperation in the college classroom*. Edina, MN: Interaction Books.

Jordan, M., & Vancil, M. (1994). *I can't accept not trying: Michael Jordan on the pursuit of excellence*. San Francisco, CA: Harper San Francisco.

Kagan, S. (2009). *Kagan cooperative learning*. San Clemente, CA: Author.

Leograndis, D. (2008). Launching the writing workshop: A step-by step guide in photographs. New York: Scholastic.

Marzano, R.J. (2006). *Classroom assessment and grading that work*. Alexandria, VA: ASCD.

McIntosh, E., & Peck, M. (2005). *Multisensory strategies: Lessons and classroom management techniques to reach and teach all learners*. New York: Scholastic.

Merz, A. (2009). Teaching for mathematical dispositions as well as for understanding: The difference between reacting to and advocating for dispositional learning. *Journal of Educational Thought, 43*(1), 65–78.

Monroe, E., & Orme, M. (2002). Developing mathematical vocabulary. *Preventing School Failure: Alternative Education for Children and Youth, 46*(3), pp. 139–142.

National Centre for Excellence in the Teaching of Mathematics. (2014). Progression in subtraction. www.ncetm.org.uk/resources/40532

National Council of Teachers of Mathematics. (2000). Principles and standards for school mathematics. Reston, VA: Author.

National Council of Teachers of Mathematics. (2002). Principles and standards for school mathematics. Reston, VA: Author.

National Governors Association Center for Best Practices & Council of Chief State School Officers. (2010). Common Core State Standards for Mathematics. Washington, DC: Author.

National Mathematics Advisory Panel. (2008). *Foundations for Success: The Final Report of the National Mathematics Advisory Panel*. Washington, DC: U.S. Department of Education.

National Research Council. (2001). *Adding it up: Helping children learn mathematics*. In J. Kilpatrick, J. Swafford, & B. Findell (Eds.), *Mathematics learning study committee, center for education, division of behavioral and social sciences and education.* Washington, DC: National Academy Press.

Neuschwander, C. (1998). *Amanda Bean's amazing dream.* Sausalito, CA: Math Solutions.

Newton, R. (2013). *Guided math in action: Building each student's mathematical proficiency with small-group instruction.* New York: Routledge.

Newton, R. (2014). Math fluency PowerPoint. Several conferences.

Pretsky, M. (2001). On the horizon. *MCB University Press, 9*(5).

Price, A. (2003). *Establishing a mathematical community of practice in the primary classroom. European research in mathematics education III.* Oxford: Oxford University Press. www.dm.unipi.it/~didattica/ CERME3/proceedings/Groups/TG8/TG8_Price_cerme3.pdf

Richardson, K. (2011). What is the distinction between a lesson and a number talk? *Math Perspectives.* www.mathperspectives.com/pdf_ docs/mp_lesson_ntalks_distinction.pdf

Russell, D., & Hunter, M. (2005). Planning effective instruction: Lesson design. In B.A. Marlowe, & A.S. Canestrari (Eds.), *Educational psychology in context; readings for future teachers* (pp. 3–12). Thousand Oaks, CA: Sage.

Scheuer, K. (2014). *A bug and a wish.* Houston, TX: Strategic Book. https:// karenscheuer.wordpress.com/2014/08/20/ welcome-to-a-bug-and-a-wish/

Shepard, L., Hammerness, K., Darling-Hammond, L., & Rust, F. (2005). Assessment. In L. Darling-Hammond & J. Bransford (Eds.), *Preparing teachers for a changing world* (pp. 275–326). San Francisco, CA: Jossey-Bass.

Spangler, R. (2010). *Strategies for teaching whole number computation: Using error analysis for intervention and analysis.* Alexandria, VA: ASCD.

Tomlinson, C.A. (1999). *The differentiated classroom: Responding to the needs of all learners.* Alexandria, VA: ASCD.

Vygotsky, L. (1978). *Mind in society: The development of higher mental processes.* Cambridge, MA: Harvard University Press.

Wiggins, G.P., & McTighe, J. (2005). *Understanding by design* (expanded 2nd ed.). Alexandria, VA: ASCD.

Williams, D. (2011). *Embedded formative assessment.* Bloomington, IN: Solution Tree Press.

Williams, H.H. (n.d.). Inspiring quotations for teachers and volunteers. Literacy Connections. www.literacyconnections.com/Quotations. php#sthash.7SbxHoC8.dpuf

Yackel, E., & Cobb, P. (1996). Sociomathematical norms, argumentation, and autonomy in mathematics. *Journal for Research in Mathematics Education, 27*(4), 458–477.